Labrador Retrievers

Edited by the Staff of T.F.H. Publications

Cover: Labs from Rocky Creek Labradors, owned by Geraldine and Kathryn Mines, Pompton Plains, New Jersey. Photo by Isabelle Francais.

Poster **A**: Yellow Labrador Retriever from Cedar Hill Kennels, owned by Thomas and Barbara Feneis, Chocolate Labrador Retrievers from Highland Kennels, Howell, New Jersey, owned by Lillian and George Knobloch, practicing in a pond in Freehold Township. Photo by Vince Serbin.

Poster **B**: A good Labrador Retriever must know how to present and hold a bird without damaging or even ruffling the bird's feathers.

Poster **C**: Yellow Labrador Retriever from Cedar Hill Kennels, owned by Thomas and Barbara Feneis. Chocolate and Black Labrador Retrievers from Highland Kennels, Howell, New Jersey, owned by Lillian and George Knobloch. Three color varieties of the breed (yellow, chocolate, and black). Photo by Vince Serbin.

Distributed in the UNITED STATES by T.F.H. Publications, Inc., 211 West Sylvania Avenue, Neptune City, NJ 07753; in CANADA by H & L Pet Supplies Inc., 27 Kingston Crescent, Kitchener, Ontario N2B 2T6; Rolf C. Hagen Ltd., 3225 Sartelon Street, Montreal 382 Quebec; in ENGLAND by T.F.H. Publications Limited, 4 Kier Park, Ascot, Berkshire SL5 7DS; in AUSTRALIA AND THE SOUTH PACIFIC by T.F.H. (Australia) Pty. Ltd., Box 149, Brookvale 2100 N.S.W., Australia; in NEW ZEALAND by Ross Haines & Son, Ltd., 18 Monmouth Street, Grey Lynn, Auckland 2 New Zealand; in SINGAPORE AND MALAYSIA by MPH Distributors (S) Pte., Ltd., 601 Sims Drive, # 03/07/21, Singapore 1438; in the PHILIPPINES by Bio-Research, 5 Lippay Street, San Lorenzo Village, Makati Rizal; in SOUTH AFRICA by Multipet Pty. Ltd., 30 Turners Avenue, Durban 4001. Published by T.F.H. Publications Inc. Manufactured in the United States of America by T.F.H. Publications, Inc.

Contents

The Labrador Retriever is an affectionate, intelligent breed of dog. He loves family life and is quick to learn and obey commands. The Lab is also easy to care for as the breed requires little grooming.

Origin and History

According to many authorities, the forebears of the Labrador were produced in Newfoundland. Authorities generally agree that the breed descended from the St. John's variety of water dog, but attempts to further trace the lineage have failed to produce any coinciding theories.

One school claims they were brought to Newfoundland by the fishermen of Devon, when they first invaded and settled the land. Another group believes they originated in North America, while still a third asserts they were of Asiatic descent.

The Labrador is supposed to have performed many useful services for the fishermen of Newfoundland— carrying ropes between boats, towing dories, and helping gather up fishnets. On several occasions he was even credited with saving crew members from watery deaths. The Labrador's stout heart and his faculty for performing numerous and varied tasks earned him a place on many a fishing boat.

Labradors in England

The first Labrador was brought to England in the early 1820s, but the breed's reputation had spread to the English shore long beforehand. As the story goes, the Earl of Malmesbury saw a Labrador on a fishing boat and immediately made arrangements with certain traders to have some imported. These first Labradors so impressed the Earl with their genius for retrieving that he devoted his entire kennel to developing and stabilizing the breed. It was not long before many others realized their worth and followed suit; unfortunately, in their enthusiasm they gave little thought to keeping the breed pure. However, the Malmesbury strain retained its purity for many years. Eventually, a combination of the Newfoundland dog tax and the English quarantine laws brought importing practically to a standstill. Interbreeding became necessary as a means of acquiring "fresh blood." In most cases this activity was restricted to the use of the curly coated and flat-coated retrievers and various breeds of water spaniels. Due to the fact that the breed was very old, its characteristics remained predominant throughout.

Finally, in 1903, the Labrador was recognized by the English Kennel Club, but at that time no definite standard of conformation was agreed upon. Fortunately for the breed, its followers were primarily interested in the development of working qualities. Unhampered by a

Origin and History

standard, they were able to continue their breeding schemes, which included occasional outcrosses, and were responsible for producing the multi-purpose dog that is our present-day Labrador Retriever.

According to records, the Labrador's first appearance in the show ring took place as early as 1860. Strangely enough, this was long before the breed received its official nod from the Kennel Club. There seems to be only one plausible explanation for this phenomenon: the old law of supply and demand. It is said that King George V had a great deal to do with awakening national interest in the breed.

Then as now, the majority of the Labrador's followers attributed little importance to success in the show ring. They measured value by the ability to deliver in the field. As a means of discerning their Labrador's respective merits, small groups of enthusiasts started to hold retriever trials in 1880. Over a period of time, the interest and the entries grew considerably. As a result of this increased competition, breeders redoubled their efforts to refine and strengthen the Labrador's valuable qualities, each striving to outdo the other. This healthy competition produced the strong foundation that

is responsible for the proficient working ability of the breed today.

Labradors in the United States

Americans knew little of the Labrador's true usefulness until after World War I. At that time they gradually began to be imported, but it was not until the middle 1930s that they gained any sort of widespread acclaim. Retriever field trials were largely responsible for the rapid spread of the breed's popularity in the United States. Once the Labrador had the chance to demonstrate his capabilities before the public, his reputation and numbers grew quickly.

The breed has made a highly successful trial record in the United States. For example, during one 20-year period, Labradors placed first in 520 out of the 637 trials open to all breeds of retrievers and Irish Water Spaniels. They have gained the coveted title of National Retriever Champion for twelve out of the first sixteen years it was in existence. Little known before the 1930s, the Labrador has already taken an unchallenged lead in the retriever field and today is steadily climbing to a well-earned place among the country's leading breeds.

Official Breed Standards

The standard of a breed is the criterion by which the appearance (and to a certain extent, the temperament) of any given dog is made subject, as far as possible, to objective measurement. Basically the standard for any breed is a definition of the perfect dog, to which all specimens of the breed are compared; the degree of excellence of the appearance of a given dog for conformation show purposes is in direct proportion to the dog's agreement with the requirements of the standard for its breed. Necessarily, of course, a certain amount of subjective evaluation is involved because of the wording of the standard itself and because of the factors introduced through the agency of the completely human judging apparatus. Breed standards are always subject to change through review by the national breed club for each dog, so it is always wise to keep up with developments in a breed by checking the publications of your national kennel club.

Following is the official standard for the Labrador Retriever as approved by the American Kennel Club. Following the A.K.C. standard is a discussion of the standard recognized by the Kennel Club of Great Britain.

The A.K.C. Standard

General Appearance: The general appearance of the Labrador should be that of a strongly built, short-coupled, very active dog. He should be fairly wide over the loins, and strong and muscular in the hindquarters. The coat should be close, short, dense and free from feather.

Head: The skull should be wide, giving brain room; there should be a slight stop, i.e. the brow should be slightly pronounced, so that the skull is not absolutely in a straight line with the nose. The head should be clean-cut and free from fleshy cheeks. The jaws should be long and powerful and free from snipiness; the nose should be wide and the nostrils well developed. Teeth should be strong and regular, with a level mouth. The ears should hang moderately close to the head, rather far back; should be set somewhat low and not be large and heavy. The eyes should be of medium size, expressing great intelligence and good temper, and can be brown, yellow or black, but brown or black is preferred.

Neck and Chest: The neck should be medium length, powerful and not throaty. The shoulders should be long and sloping. The

Official Breed Standards

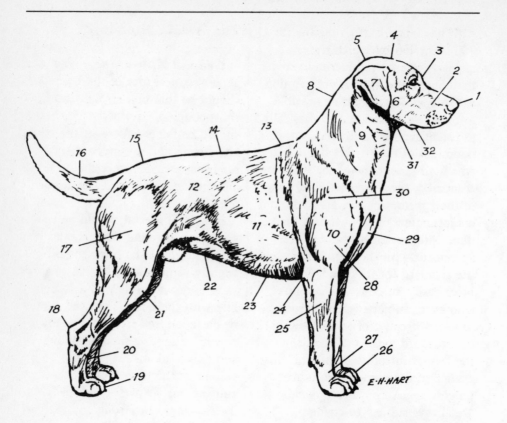

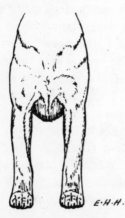

*Above: The external anatomy of the Labrador:
1. Nose. 2. Muzzle. 3. Stop. 4. Skull. 5. Occi-
put. 6. Cheek. 7. Ear. 8. Crest of neck. 9.
Neck. 10. Shoulder. 11. Ribs. 12. Loin. 13.
Withers. 14. Back. 15. Croup. 16. Tail or
stern. 17. Thigh. 18. Hock joint. 19. Rear feet.
20. Metatarsus. 21. Stifle. 22. Abdomen. 23.
Chest. 24. Elbow. 25. Foreleg. 26. Front feet.
27. Pastern. 28. Upper arm. 29. Forechest. 30.
Shoulder blade. 31. Throat latch. 32. Lip corner.*

Left: An excellent Lab front.

Official Breed Standards

chest must be of good width and depth, the ribs well sprung and the loins wide and strong, stifles well turned, and the hindquarters well developed and of great power.

Legs and Feet: The legs must be straight from the shoulder to ground, and the feet compact with toes well arched, and pads well developed; the hocks should be well bent, and the dog must neither be cowhocked nor be too wide behind; in fact, he must stand and move true all round on legs and feet. Legs should be of medium length, showing good bone and muscle, but not so short as to be out of balance with rest of body. In fact, a dog well balanced in all points is preferable to one with outstanding good qualities and defects.

Tail: The tail is a distinctive feature of the breed; it should be very thick towards the base, gradually tapering towards the tip, of medium length, should be free from any feathering, and should be clothed thickly all round with the Labrador's short, thick, dense coat, thus giving the peculiar "rounded" appearance which has been described as the "otter" tail. The tail may be carried gaily but should not curl over the back.

Coat: The coat is another very distinctive feature; it should be short, very dense and without wave, and should give a fairly hard feeling to the hand.

Color: The colors are black, yellow, or chocolate and are evaluated as follows:

(a) **Blacks:** All black, with a small white spot on chest permissible. Eyes to be of medium size, expressing intelligence and good temper, preferably brown or hazel, although black or yellow is permissible.

(b) **Yellows:** Yellows may vary in color from fox-red to light cream with variations in the shading of the coat on ears, the underparts of the dog, or beneath the tail. A small

---

Excellent hindquarters on a Lab.

Official Breed Standards

white spot on chest is permissible.
Eye coloring and expression should
be the same as that of the blacks,
with black or dark brown eye rims.
The nose should also be black or
dark brown, although "fading" to
pink in winter weather is not
serious. A "Dudley" nose, (pink
without pigmentation) should be
penalized.

(c) **Chocolates:** Shades ranging
from light sedge to chocolate. A
small white spot on chest is
permissible. Eyes to be light brown
to clear yellow. Nose and eye-rim
pigmentation dark brown or liver
colored. "Fading" to pink in winter
weather not serious. "Dudley" nose
should be penalized.

Movement: Movement should be
free and effortless. The forelegs
should be strong and true, and
correctly placed. Watching a dog
move towards one, there should be
no signs of elbows being out in
front, but neatly held to the body
with legs not too close together, and
moving straight forward without
pacing or weaving. Upon viewing
the dog from the rear, one should
get the impression that the hind
legs, which should be well muscled
and not cowhocked, move as nearly
parallel as possible, with hocks
doing their full share of work and
flexing well, thus giving the

appearance of power and strength.

*Approximate Weights of Dogs
and Bitches in Working
Condition:* Dogs—60 to 75 pounds;
bitches—55 to 70 pounds.

Height at Shoulders:
Dogs—22½ inches to 24½ inches;
bitches—21½ inches to 23½ inches.

The British Standard

The Kennel Club (Great Britain)
standard for the Labrador Retriever
is essentially the same as the
American Kennel Club standard;
there are, however, certain
differences that are important
enough for specific mention. If your
dog is of British registry or if you
plan to show him in competitions
that are under the jurisdiction of the
Kennel Club you should especially
note the following variances in the
requirements (and also obtain a copy
of the complete official standard).

Head: The jaws should be
medium length.

Size: Desired height for dogs, 22
to 22½ inches; for bitches, 21½ to
22 inches.

Faults: Undershot or overshot
mouth; lack of undercoat; bad
action; feathering; snipiness on the
head; large or heavy ears; cowhocked; tail curled over back.

10

Temperament and Personality

The reason for the Labrador's swift rise in popularity is that over the years he has consistently proved his worth in all fields and truly earned the title "all around" dog.

One of the most predominant characteristics of the Labrador is a strong desire to please. This quality has done much to enhance the breed's popularity. Coupled with a high degree of native intelligence, it equips the Labrador to fulfill the roles of hunter, retriever, companion, pet and watchdog. This desire to please makes the Labrador a willing and eager pupil, a dog that enjoys learning and is a pleasure to teach.

A Devoted Worker

By far the most exciting of the Labrador's qualities is his inherent working ability. This all-important factor has been maintained and strengthened over the years by careful and selective breeding. So strong is the Labrador's natural inclination for retrieving that it is manifested when a puppy is still under three months of age.

Another endearing characteristic of the breed is untiring devotion to people. The Labrador thrives on human company and companionship; he has the rare ability of being able to be everybody's friend and still maintain an undying allegiance to his master.

The Labrador has the uncanny and most admirable quality of being able to adapt himself to all sorts of situations and surroundings. His devotion and patience make him a trusted playmate for children. He joins in their games with enthusiasm and thoroughly enjoys what you and I would consider mauling. At the same time, he is perfectly able to take care of himself by simply evacuating the area if things get too rough. Somehow, in each instance, the Labrador seems to grasp almost instinctively what is desired and to willingly apply himself in that direction.

Few other breeds can match the Labrador for perseverance and courage. His reputation was founded on his ability to withstand the hardships of a day's shoot. Whether it is retrieving ducks in icy water on a cold winter day or hunting pheasants in honeysuckle groves, hedgerows, briar patches, and other likely spots, the Labrador performs his task like a trooper. How much wounded game would have been lost if it were not for the Labrador's excellent scenting powers and perseverance! Any duck hunter

Temperament and Personality

Labradors excel in field trials, where dogs are judged according to their ability and style on following a game trail or on finding and retrieving game; all Lab owners can get a thrill out of seeing this breed perform in this competition.

knows the trouble strong wounded game can cause, but the Labrador does not give up. Certain members of the breed have been known to carry on hot pursuit for over an hour.

The Labrador's Appearance

The Labrador's body and coat fit him so well for both indoor and outdoor life that they seem to have been designed for that purpose by a master craftsman. He has a rugged appearance, standing about two feet high, being fairly long and very solid in body, with a good head, thick neck, deep chest, and well-developed legs. Even his tail contributes to his work. While he is swimming it acts as a rudder, and when he is working the upland it waves like a flag, signaling when he is making game. His "polished" coat sheds water quickly and protects him from burrs and briars, enabling him to get through the thickest of cover.

All told, the Labrador's many admirable qualities render him truly a dog of distinction. So long as there remains a person who values loyalty and courage, the Labrador will have a friend.

Exercise and Environment

Although the Labrador has a wonderful ability to adjust himself to almost any sort of condition or surroundings, there are a few essentials necessary to his development and well-being that we as owners and dog lovers must grant him.

Exercise

To fit him for his role of hunter and retriever, the Labrador has been endowed with a great amount of strength and stamina. Whether you plan to hunt your dog or merely utilize his capacity as a friend and companion, you must see to it that he gets ample opportunity for exercise.

If you live in a city or large town and your only means of exercising are leash and collar promenades, the Labrador is not the dog for you. He was not meant for that sort of existence any more than the proverbial fish deprived of water. To maintain health and happiness and properly develop his body, the Labrador must have at least fifteen minutes of unrestricted exercise twice a day.

1. Limited choke. 2. Pliable leash, 6 feet long. 3. Chain choke collar. 4. Wooden dumbbell. 5. Long leash.

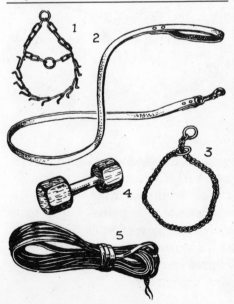

General Care

The Labrador provides a bottomless source of companionship, pleasure, and love. In return, the least we can do is to protect his rights by ensuring his physical and mental comfort. The basis of mental comfort is simple: it is merely a mutual understanding and respect. The main dangers to it are:
1. Loss of temper, resulting in harsh treatment.
2. Punishing the dog for something he does not understand.

3. Attempting to teach him too many things too soon, and for periods too long in time.
4. Allowing children to abuse him.

Sleeping Quarters

Proper sleeping quarters have a great deal to do with maintaining a dog's health. Of primary importance, whether inside or outside, is that the bed be free from drafts and dampness. If your Labrador sleeps in the house, he is probably not subjected to this sort of danger. But if he lives outside, make sure his house is raised off the ground. This is easily done by nailing a couple of two-by-fours to the base. In cold weather, extra bedding and a double flap of burlap nailed over the entrance will take care of the insulating problem. If you make it a practice to feed twice daily in winter, the Labrador will be able to generate enough body heat to keep himself and his house warm throughout the day.

In the summer, special care should be taken to see that there is a shady spot in the yard at all times of the day. A platform about a foot and a half high will provide the necessary shade and also give him a

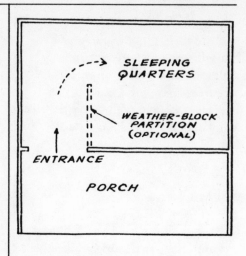

The floor plan (above) for a good doghouse (below).

place to lie when the ground is cold and wet. If you must take him in the car with you, make sure to leave windows at least partially open so there is cross ventilation, and park in a spot that is shady and will remain shady for the duration of your absence.

14

Your New Puppy

Now, assuming that you have decided that this is the right breed for you, there remain the questions of which puppy to choose, where to purchase him, and the general management of the puppy once he is in your home.

Sex and Age

This is no place to undertake a "battle of the sexes." Since no dog should run loose, a female, during the brief sex-vulnerable intervals of estrus twice a year, will be chaperoned whenever outdoors; or it is relatively easy to keep her safely confined or to board her with your veterinarian or at a reliable kennel. All her life she can alternate between indoor and outdoor bathroom facilities. A female usually is more gently affectionate, particularly with young children. On the other hand, a male, after he reaches an age to lift his leg, must be let or taken outside to relieve himself four times every single day, no matter what the inconvenience. He may display embarrassing interest in the sex of other dogs he encounters; leave his "calling card" on every post, tree, shrub or hydrant; and although housebroken at home, cannot always be trusted in unfamiliar private or public premises. No one can make this decision for you.

As to age, two and a half to three months is young enough. By that age, a puppy is weaned and independent of his mother's care and company, day or night. He is well adapted to his diet and a convenient meal schedule. He is old enough for vaccinations against distemper and other contagious diseases (in fact, a vaccination program may have already been started for the puppy by his seller), and he is at the most responsive age to begin to understand and heed the lessons of housebreaking. A younger puppy requires frequent attention, almost foster-mothering, which cannot be delegated to children or neglected even for a few hours. A lower price at a lower age is no bargain.

Pet versus Show Prospect

It is well to define in your own mind the purpose for which you want a dog and to convey this to the breeder. A great deal of disappointment and dissatisfaction can be avoided by a meeting of the minds between seller and buyer.

Your New Puppy

Although every well-bred, healthy member of the breed makes an ideal companion and pet, actual pet-stock is usually the least expensive of the purebred registered stock. The person who asks for a pet pays a pet-geared price for the animal. Pet stock is least expensive because these dogs are deemed unsuitable for breeding or exhibition in comparison to the standard of perfection for the breed. Generally, only skilled breeders and judges can point out the structural differences between pet- and show-quality dogs.

If you are planning to show your dog, make this clear to the breeder and he will aid you in selecting the best possible specimen of the breed. A show-quality dog may be more expensive than one meant for a pet, but it will be able to stand up to show-ring competition.

Where to Buy Your Puppy

Once you have decided on the particular breed that you want for your pet, your task is to find that one special dog from among several outlets. Buying a well-bred, healthy dog is your foremost concern. By doing a little research in the various dog magazines and newspapers, you can locate the names and addresses

Captions for color photos on pages 17 through 24:
Page 17: Labrador Retrievers are trained to retrieve on land as well as in water. This one is owned by Lillian Knobloch. Photo by Vince Serbin. Page 18: A black Labrador Retriever guarding the catch of the day, a mallard duck. Page 19: A Driftwood Kennels' Labrador Retriever, with plastic dummy, swimming eagerly toward the shore. Photo by Vince Serbin. Pages 20-21: Appearance of a dog embryo after 55 days of development. Dogs are born between 58 and 63 days of gestation. Page 22: When training is completed, these Labs from Driftwood Kennels will no longer fight over a plastic dummy or a retrieved bird. Photo by Vince Serbin. Page 23: Notice that the puppies are both chocolate and black. The sire was a black carrying the chocolate gene; the dam is chocolate. Chocolate is recessive to black, black is a pure dominant, and yellow a true recessive to both black and chocolate. Photo by Vince Serbin. Page 24: Another Lab from Driftwood Kennels watching his trainer closely during retrieving exercises. Photo by Vince Serbin.

Captions for color photos on pages 57 through 64:
Page 57: Appearance of a typical Labrador Retriever head. Owned by George and Lillian Knobloch, Highland Kennels, Howell, New Jersey. Photo by Vince Serbin. Page 58: (Top) Eleven developing embryos can be counted in this photo of the reproductive duct (uterus) of a dog. (Bottom) A very immature embryo. Page 59: (Top and bottom) Uterus of dog with embryos in two different stages of development, more advanced stage in the bottom photo. Pages 60-61: A Labrador Retriever is a very intelligent dog and can excel both as a show dog and a field dog. This one is owned by Highland Kennels. Photo by Vince Serbin. Page 62: (Top) Note the umbilical cord attached to this embryo. (Bottom) An embryo with placenta and unbroken embryonic sac. Page 63: (Top) An embryo with the sac removed. (Bottom) Note the important blood vessels passing through the umbilical cord in this embryo. Page 64: A yellow Labrador Retriever from Cedarhill Kennel, owned by Thomas and Barbara Feneis, Freehold, New Jersey. Photo by Vince Serbin.

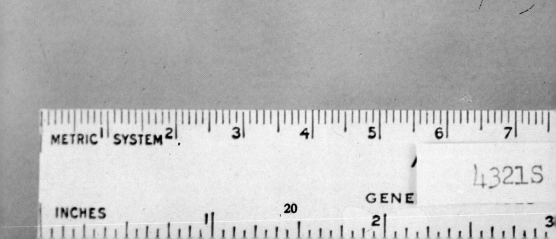

55 Days

ST. LOUIS 8, MO.

21

DEVISED BY J. W. FEBER, W. P.

Your New Puppy

of breeders and kennels in your area that are known for breeding quality animals. Your national dog club will also furnish you with addresses of people to contact who are knowledgeable about your chosen breed.

Your local pet shop, although necessarily restricted from carrying all breeds in stock, may sometimes be able to supply quality puppies on demand. Due to the exorbitant amount of space and time needed to properly rear puppies, pet shops generally prefer to assist owners by supplying all the tools and equipment needed in the raising and training of the puppies. The pet shop proprietor, if unable to obtain a dog for you, can often refer you to a reputable kennel with which he has done business before.

Selection

When you do pick out a puppy as a pet, don't be hasty; the longer you study puppies, the better you will understand them. Make it your transcendent concern to select only one that radiates good health and spirit and is lively on his feet, whose eyes are bright, whose coat shines, and who comes forward eagerly to make and to cultivate your acquaintance. Don't fall for any shy little darling that wants to retreat to his bed or his box, or plays coy behind other puppies or people, or hides his head under your arm or jacket appealing to your protective instinct. *Pick the puppy who forthrightly picks you! The feeling of attraction should be mutual!*

Documents

Now, a little paper work is in order. When you purchase a purebred puppy, you should receive a transfer of ownership, registration material, and other "papers" (a list of the immunization shots, if any, the puppy may have been given; a note on whether or not the puppy has been wormed; a diet and feeding schedule to which the puppy is accustomed) and you are welcomed as a fellow owner to a long, pleasant association with a most lovable pet, and more (news)paper work.

Bringing the Puppy Home

If you take the puppy home by car, protect him from drafts, particularly in cold weather. Wrapped in a towel and carried in the arms or lap of a passenger, the puppy usually will make the trip without mishap. If the pup starts to drool and to squirm, stop the car for

Your New Puppy

a few minutes. Have newspapers handy in case of car-sickness. A covered carton lined with newspapers provides protection for puppy and car, if you are driving alone. Avoid excitement and unnecessary handling of the puppy on arrival. A puppy is a very small "package" to be making complete change of surroundings and company, and he needs frequent rest and refreshment to renew his vitality.

Let the puppy set his own pace for the first few days. Give him the liberty to thoroughly investigate the strange new world in which he finds himself. Allow him to familiarize himself with its inhabitants in his own good time. After all, there will be a whole lifetime for affection and play. The most important thing now is to make him feel relaxed and "at home."

During the course of the puppy's introductory tour, it is more than likely that one or more wet spots will mysteriously appear. Let them remain a mystery for the time being. The puppy has enough to do in getting used to his new life and the missing security of his mother and litter mates without having to contend with a reprimand to further tarnish his already dim view of the situation.

It usually does not take a long time for a Labrador to adjust to his new home.

A Place of His Own

At the first signs of tiredness the puppy should be escorted to his bed. A box or a basket will serve the purpose well, as long as it has sides in order to be completely draft free. A wire enclosure, about two feet by four feet, around the bed is advantageous for three reasons. First of all, it will teach the puppy that he has to spend some time by himself. Secondly, it makes the cleaning task easy—just a case of removing soiled newspapers and adding fresh ones. Last of all, it will

Your New Puppy

keep him out of trouble when there is work to be done and no one available to act as chaperon. There should always be a few playthings left in the pen.

A well-wrapped hot water bottle and a wind-up clock placed in the bed at night should solve the howling problem. The warmth of the bottle and the constant noise of the clock represent companionship to a puppy.

When and What to Feed

Mealtime for the puppy must be absolutely regular. From the time of weaning to three months, puppies should be fed four times a day: in the morning, at noon, during early evening, and at bedtime. You can set the exact times best suited to your own convenience; but once you have laid the plan, stick to it. For the first few days try to duplicate the menu that the pup has been used to. It will help to put him at ease.

Breakfast should be warm milk, mixed with farina or any one of the prepared breakfast cereals. Lunch and dinner should consist of puppy meal, soaked until soft in warm broth, milk, or water, with a generous supply of ground or

chopped meat mixed in before feeding. The bedtime meal should be similar to breakfast.

You will find that canned milk is more valuable in content and less expensive than the regular variety. The meat can be beef or lamb, either canned or fresh, but it must be chopped or ground, as the puppy is not yet sufficiently equipped to tackle the chewing problem. A teaspoonful of cod-liver oil and one of bone meal should be given daily. If you have any leftover vegetables, by all means include them in the meals. They are a rich source of vitamins and minerals to bolster the daily supply. Eggs are another vitamin source; add one (the raw yolk alone; or if given whole, the egg should be cooked) to a meal at least three times weekly.

It is practically impossible to prescribe the amount to be fed; it varies with the individual puppy. The only foolproof method is to measure by what is consumed and add or subtract accordingly. Remember that as the puppy grows he will require more food.

From the third to the sixth month, a puppy requires only three daily meals—breakfast, lunch, and dinner. Between six months and one year, feeding can be cut down to two meals a day, morning and

27

Your New Puppy

evening. Stop the milk and cereal, substituting the old lunch menu for breakfast. When the puppy is one year old, he is physically matured and needs only one meal a day. It is a good idea to feed him at noon, as this will give him ample time to relieve himself and ensure a comfortable night for all concerned.

Before the puppy is three months old his water supply should be somewhat restricted; offer him a drink between meals, removing the dish when he has had enough. Otherwise, he is apt to finish it all and have no appetite for food. For the older puppy, be sure to have a supply of drinking water within easy reach at all times.

Teaching the Labrador Puppy

There are a few basic principles that should be well understood before anyone attempts to teach a puppy anything.

1. The Labrador puppy is born with an inherent desire to please. If he does wrong, it is very probable that he does not understand what is wanted.
2. His only means of learning is memory; the only method for teaching him is repetition.
3. The greatest tool for training is praise. If you make the lessons a game and you both have fun, your task will be accomplished more rapidly.
4. Loss of patience or harsh treatment will only confuse and disillusion the puppy, making your job a longer and more difficult one.

Housetraining a Labrador Puppy

By nature, Labradors are not unclean creatures. The last thing they want is to foul their own house. Unfortunately, they will unless they are taught not to.

Actually, it is a very simple matter to house train a puppy. The most important thing is to take the puppy outside immediately after each meal. The first time, allow him to pick the spot, and each time thereafter head for the same location. It won't be long before he associates the place with the job to be done. Give him at least three other opportunities to relieve himself during the course of the day. Each time, stay out until he has accomplished his mission and then praise him. This schedule should fill his needs, but if you find it lacking, try airing him every hour.

Your New Puppy

A puppy will seldom make a mess without giving ample warning. The commonest danger signals are: 1. Wandering around, sniffing the floor. 2. Moving in circles. 3. Whining.

If your puppy shows any one of the signals, pick him up quickly and take him out.

If by chance he slips away and makes a mess unnoticed, take him back to the scene, point to the spot, and repeat firmly, "no, no." Then take him outside. If he persists in fouling the house after he has been with you for a month or six weeks, accompany your firm "No, no" with taps on the hindquarters, using a rolled newspaper. It serves the purpose well, as puppies hate the noise and it cannot possibly do them any physical harm.

Do not get the notion that he can now last overnight. This is not possible until he is at least six months old. Most likely he will mess in his pen every night. Do not scold him. After all, he did not have the opportunity to do otherwise.

Collar and Leash Training

Now as to general management, immediately put on him a small leather collar and have a leash to go with it. He probably won't notice the collar at all; but if he does, and seems to fight it, let him fight it and pay no attention. He'll get used to it quickly. Leave it on all the time. Whenever he goes outside, snap a leash onto the collar. City or country, always take your dog out with collar and leash. This is his first taste of discipline. And discipline is not punishment—it is training!

All training is done on the leash. He may buck and plunge a bit at first, finding himself unable to run around at will. Hold the leash firmly, but let it "give" a lot for the first few days. Do not start him off with the chain collar. Such a collar is ideal later, but it is painful and even dangerous on a young puppy. Gradually teach him to walk quietly on the leash, always on your left side. Hold the leash in such a way to prevent him from running ahead of you or crossing your path. By all means, start his leash and collar work as soon as you get him. Don't start his formal training until he is five or six months old, or maybe a little older, depending on the dog himself. Meanwhile, he is learning what "No" means, and he is learning to come when called. Always speak his name first, followed by the command "Come."

And make it a command, but slap your knees to encourage him at first. Study your training book now, even though you won't start regular training for months.

To Spay or Not to Spay

To spay a female dog (past tense, *spayed)* is to remove both ovaries from the dog surgically, thus rendering it impossible for the dog ever to have puppies or periods of "heat " or "season."

Spaying usually does not affect the dog's personality or characteristic joy in living. Granted, there is a tendency to get fat, but this situation is easily regulated by proper feeding.

To anyone not interested in breeding dogs but who wants a fine companion and housedog, the spayed female has no superior. Always beautiful anyway, she is keen, smart, and lively.

Special Care for the Brood Bitch

The female usually comes in heat for the first time between the ages of seven and 12 months. And allowing for some variations in individual dogs, the female will come in heat roughly twice a year, once in the spring and once in the fall, or thereabouts.

If you live in the city, the heat period will cause you little if any inconvenience, since, in the city, dogs are more apt to be leashed or more carefully controlled than dogs in the suburbs and country. But the safe rule, to guard against accidental breeding, is to keep your female always on a lead throughout the entire heat period. As for the droplets of discharge around the house, they are odorless and may easily be removed by wiping with a damp cloth.

In the country or suburbs, you may have somewhat of a problem. Again, take your female outside only on a leash and keep her close beside you. If possible, walk her a little way from the house to relieve herself, keeping a sharp lookout for visiting males. Some males are extremely fast operators; and unless you are very careful, especially from the seventh or eighth day on, you may have an unwanted breeding before you know it. In this instance, once such a breeding has begun, there is absolutely nothing you can do about it. Attempted separation of the two animals will result in serious injury to both.

Retrieving

This phase of training should not be started until the dog is over six months old and should not include more than two or three retrieves a day for the first few months. There are two things that must be accomplished early in a Labrador's career. First, his work must become the most exciting thing in his life, and secondly, his hunting instinct must be developed. There is only one way in which these things can be satisfactorily established, and that is by the strict rationing of daily work allotments.

The act of retrieving must be associated with a command. Whether you choose "Get back!" "Get out!" or the dog's name as your signal, it must be accompanied by a hand motion in the direction of the fall and be used before each retrieve.

Boat fenders are the most satisfactory things to use for the early lessons. They are the perfect shape, come in varying weights, and do for land and water retrieves. About six inches of clothesline tied on to the end of the fender will make it easier to manipulate and greatly increase the distance it can be thrown.

The first step is to introduce the puppy to the training dummy. This should be made as exciting as possible. A playful voice and teasing actions build up the suspense. When his enthusiasm reaches the boiling point, hurl the dummy out about twenty feet. The instant he reaches it, start blowing the "Come!" whistle, at the same time clapping your hands and running away. (These antics are necessary to ensure a speedy return.) Once he has has caught up to you, reach down and take the dummy gently. Praise him thoroughly and then repeat the action, this time throwing it a bit farther.

For the first few days the lessons should take place on bare ground or a lawn. As soon as the puppy comprehends the retrieving principle, you can move to a spot that has just enough cover to conceal the dummy. From now on, the puppy should be held and not given the command to retrieve until the dummy hits the ground. Gradually increase the distance of the retrieves when his past performance shows that he has mastered the present length. The same principle applies to the use of higher and thicker types of cover.

If in the course of training he should have trouble finding the dummy and head back toward you, ignore him. Nine times out of ten, as soon as he sees that help is not

Retrieving

When training for water retrieves, an experienced water dog can serve as a good example for your pup to follow.

forthcoming, he will return to the job. This is important, because it is the only way to develop perseverance. Once he gets accustomed to receiving help, he will ask for it whenever the going gets tough. Needless to say, this is an undesirable trait and most difficult to overcome once it has been established.

Introduction to Water: Before the puppy is asked to do any kind of work in the water, he should have a pleasant and gradual introduction.

About the most successful way to accomplish this is to enlist the aid of a good water dog; throw a dummy and let your dog follow the other dog at will. After you have repeated this several times to everyone's satisfaction, try your dog alone on a short retrieve, releasing

him before the dummy has landed. If he fails to enter the water promptly, release the veteran again to set the example.

A great many lessons can be taught using this method. You will find that a dog, like a child, learns some things more quickly through imitation. Also, the presence of competition will increase your dog's enthusiasm and should do away with any doubts he might have concerning the new adventure.

If a reliable water dog is not available, one of several other methods can be employed. One way is to place yourself across a small stretch of water from the dog and then call him to you. Another way is to set the example yourself by wading into the water and calling your dog. You may also get into a rowboat and coax the dog to swim out to you.

Retrieving in Water: The first few times, toss the dummy close to the shore and let the puppy go after it while it is still in the air. The second he has it, start blowing your whistle furiously and moving backwards. This should avoid the possibility of his dropping it on the shore. Once he has the idea, you can follow the same length-increasing schedule as used for land work.

Retrieving

Longer Retrieves: For this purpose it is necessary to enlist the aid of a helper. Be sure the helper understands the importance of throwing high in order for the dog to mark the fall, and making a sharp noise, such as "Hey," to get the dog's attention before he throws.

Up until now, the dog has been accustomed to your throwing; with the change, the lessons must revert to bare ground. In the beginning, it is very likely that the dog will attempt to deliver the dummy to the helper. But, if you instruct him beforehand to remain motionless and double your own whistling, clapping and running antics, this can be overcome immediately.

A pup should first be introduced to water by letting him walk through a pan of water or a shallow brook. If gradually introduced to deep water, a Lab will eventually be difficult to keep out of it.

As soon as you think the dog has caught on to the change, head back to cover. At the start, shorten up on the retrieves and work into the wind. When he has progressed to the stage where he is going out ninety yards both on land and water, hunting the area of the fall until he finds the object, and returning with enthusiasm, he is ready to be steadied and taught to deliver to hand.

Steadying the Labrador: Gradually, you have been increasing the length between the time the dummy hits the ground and when you send your Labrador to retrieve. When he will sit for about five seconds without the slightest struggle and still retain his enthusiasm, he is ready to be steadied. This means sitting without being held until he gets the signal to retrieve.

Tell him firmly to sit, then signal your helper to throw. Count up to five and then send your dog. If he should move beforehand, do your utmost to catch him. If he is too fast and escapes, instruct your helper to pick up the dummy immediately. Then you can bring him back to the starting point, tell him to sit, and reprimand him. But if he gets the dummy and brings it to you, you cannot punish him because he is doing the right thing

Retrieving

(but in the wrong way). Always remember that in all forms of dog training, punishment must be administered *immediately* after the misdeed. After a while, you will be able to recognize standard signals your dog gives before he breaks, such as a slight raising of the hindquarters or straightening of the tail. On the first evidence of a signal, repeat a firm "sit" command. The average Labrador catches on to this quickly because of his thorough obedience schooling, but sometimes it is necessary to take stronger measures. A check cord attached to his collar works wonders and usually requires use only once. The method is to let the dog go a few yards at full speed and then to pull on the rope. A firm footing and a pair of gloves are useful props.

Delivering to Hand: This means that he is to hold the dummy until you take it from him. The command for this is "Fetch!" Have the dog sit; open his mouth and put in the dummy, repeating the command. If he tries to spit it out, hold his mouth closed and say "Fetch!" repeatedly. The first few times, make him hold it for only a few seconds. After the first lesson you can gradually decrease the pressure of your hands until just a few taps under the lower jaw will accomplish the purpose. When he associates the action with the command, move away from him, making him "Fetch!" on his own. Then call him to you and take the dummy, following up the action with the usual reward of praise.

Double Retrieves: Lessons must again revert to the lawn. Have your helper go out about thirty yards. He should throw first, and his dummy must fall close to where yours will fall. Send the dog at once. Give him the "Come!" whistle the second he picks up your short dummy; wait to send him for the long fall until his attention is focused in that direction. Sometimes it is necessary to have the helper rethrow the long dummy.

When the dog catches on to the fact that there are two objects to retrieve, he is often tempted to bring them both in at the same time. Your long-suffering helper should be alerted beforehand of this danger. The moment he sees the dog heading toward him with the short dummy still in his mouth, he must grab his dummy and conceal it, replacing it only after the dog is on his way back to you. Occasionally it is necessary to again resort to the check cord to convince the dog that this practice is not the proper method of approach. If this

Retrieving

A properly trained Lab will hold the retrieve in his mouth until given the command to put it in his trainer's hand.

is the case, snap on the check cord before the retrieve and remove it after he has delivered the short dummy.

After three or four lessons on the lawn the average pupil is ready for doubles in cover.

Doubles in Water: Never attempt water doubles until the dog is completely over the temptation of bringing both dummies at once. At first they should be short retrieves and thrown to fall a wide distance apart.

Introduction to the Gun: There is no excuse for having a gun-shy dog. All that is necessary are a few precautionary measures. The earlier a dog is accustomed to loud noises, the better it is. This conditioning can start in puppyhood by banging on a pan or slamming a door during mealtime. This way, loud noises will be associated with pleasure from the start.

The first time a shotgun is introduced, it should be from a distance and accompanied by something to retrieve. Gradually the distance can be decreased.

Introduction to Feathers: This should follow the same routine as the dummy introduction. A pigeon is the best bird to begin with, since it is most easily managed by a young dog. It is a good idea to fasten the wings to the body with elastic bands so that the dog will learn to take a good hold from the beginning. After he learns to handle pigeons, other game birds can be used.

Learning to Trail: A wing-clipped duck is the best bird to start with, because it has by far the strongest scent. Let the duck have about a minute head start and then lead your dog to the spot where the trail begins. Give him the command to retrieve; in the beginning, if need be, follow along behind him with

Retrieving

encouraging words. Be especially careful not to let him get in the habit of backtrailing. Gradually increase the length of the trails by letting the duck have more of a head start. When your Labrador can follow a downwind trail for a distance of seventy yards or more, he is ready for pheasants.

Introduction to Decoys: The easiest way to accustom a dog to decoys is to lay some on the lawn and walk him through them at heel. All investigations should be discouraged by firm, repeated "No's."

The next step is to toss a dummy to land beyond them, so that he must go through the decoys to retrieve. If he should grab a decoy instead of the dummy, replace it, repeating "No!", and throw the dummy again. When he ignores the decoys completely on land, repeat the exercise in the water.

Retrieving Across Water and Roads, Through Fences, Changes of Cover: All retrieving done through or across natural hazards must be

Labrador Retrievers have an inherent desire to work and they most enjoy the company of the person who trains them.

Retrieving

simply introduced. Begin with a short single. Once the dog understands and can sufficiently cope with the new problem, the distance and number of retrieves can increase.

Teaching the Dog to Take a Line and to Obey Hand Signals: This is essential knowledge for the shooting dog, for it is the only way that he can retrieve birds he has not seen fall.

Since the dog has been accustomed to getting a line to a fall from the beginning of his training, he will naturally connect the hand and voice signal with something to retrieve. But the problem is getting him to run a straight line indefinitely when he has not seen anything fall. In the early stages of learning line running, a straight stretch of road or a fence can be employed as a guide. The dummy should be placed beforehand, within plain sight of the starting point. Have the dog sit and line him out. Be sure he sees the dummy before you give him the command to retrieve. Gradually lengthen the distance of these "blind retrieves" until he will go out in a straight line for a distance of a hundred yards. When you think your dog is in the habit of running a straight line, try him in an open field without the

former guide. Shorten up on the length at first.

Hand signals are simply a branch of obedience training and can be started as soon as the dog is steady and knows his "Sit-stay," "Heel," "Sit," and "Come" to the whistle. But they must be completely divorced from field work until the dog has fully developed his marking and hunting ability.

Like early lessons in retrieving, the hand signals should begin on bare ground. Sit the dog, then walk about forty yards away from him. Throw a dummy so that it lands to the right and an equal distance between you and your Labrador. Then give him the "Come" whistle. When he has progressed about twenty yards toward you, give him the "Sit" whistle. As soon as he sits, throw your right arm out to the side and command, "Over!" By switching arms, the same routine follows for the left direction. The signal for getting directly back is an arm held straight up, accompanied by the command, "Back!"

The next step, still on bare ground, is to lay the dummies out beforehand in triangular position. Then place the dog slightly above the base of the triangle and midway between the right and left dummies. Before each signal, give the "Come"

Retrieving

whistle, and when he has advanced to the base of the triangle, the "Sit" whistle, followed in a few seconds by a hand signal. Mix up the sequence, first over right, then back, then over left, and then reversing it. Gradually lengthen the size of the triangle, until the dog is used to going fifty yards or so in one direction.

When he has thoroughly digested the hand signals and is proficient at running a line, the two can be incorporated. The "blind retrieve" should be short to start with and set up so that the wind blows across it. Line the dog well to the downwind side of the bird, and when he reaches the spot where the wind will help him, stop him with the "Sit" whistle and give him the proper "Over" signal. Once he is carrying out all the signals close in with the help of the wind, start increasing the length and including all the directional signals in one retrieve.

Teaching the Labrador to Quarter and to Flush Game: Although the Labrador is primarily a retriever, he possesses the intelligence and native ability to make a top-notch hunter. With a slight amount of prompting, most Labradors will take quite naturally to working like a spaniel. But this phase of their training must be withheld until they have become thoroughly skilled in marking, working out the area of a fall, running a line, and taking directions.

First of all, it is essential to secure the services of a reliable pigeon shot, a couple of pigeons, and a good size field with medium cover. Make sure the dog is where he cannot see any of the proceedings. Then, dizzy one of the pigeons and plant it in a thick spot of cover out about 150 yards. When you have collected your gun, friend and dog, start out in the direction of the bird; after a few yards, tell the dog to "Hie on!" When he gets about twenty yards out, stop him with the "Sit" whistle and give him the "Over" direction. Keeping him always in gun range as you walk, cast him first to one side and then the other, thus quartering the field, until you have reached the area of the planted pigeon. As he approaches the spot, sneak up and get ready to give the "Sit" whistle the second the bird is flushed. If he should ignore the whistle and chase after the bird, tell your friend to hold shot. Run out immediately and grab the dog, bring him back to the spot, repeat the command and reprimand him. But, if all goes well, let your friend shoot and the dog retrieve.

Tributes to the Breed

Anyone who has ever shot over a Labrador knows the thrill that comes from watching this dog at work. So great is the Labrador's love of his profession that his entire personality changes at just the sight of a gun being taken out of the closet. His excitement is intense, and from that first moment until departure time he never leaves his shooting partner's side by more than a few feet.

The dog's enthusiasm is so strong that it affects all those who come into contact with him, greatly increasing their enjoyment of the sport. But with this added impetus comes a conscience, for it does not take the Labrador long to wise up to the fact that you, too, have your bad days, and his subsequent disappointment will affect you far more than your own disgust.

We have a wonderful old bitch who was brought into the family as a pup. Her shooting experiences had always been with my father until, on this one day, she was loaned to another couple in the same ducking group. Their blind was on the end of a point, about half a mile distant from my father's position. Everything was in readiness well before dawn, and with the first signs of light the ducks began to move. For some reason that morning the point blind saw very little action, and to make it worse the people in it promptly muffed the few chances they had. About an hour of this was all the old bitch could stand. She waited for her chance and then slipped away. Ten minutes later a black head was in the water, approaching my unaware father's blind.

As evidence of the breed's intelligence, supersensitive nose, and devotion to masters is the following story of a Labrador who was left alone in a strange place. The incident took place on a night's stop during the return from a shooting trip. The dog was taken by car to a strange kennel, approximately three miles from the strange house. He had a good view of the road and watched his master's car until it disappeared. During the night he succeeded in climbing out of his pen and making his way to the house, but he had no way of getting inside. So he tried to do the next best thing, get into the car. Here again his efforts were thwarted, as it was locked. He finally settled for sleeping under the car, satisfied that was the nearest to his master he could get.

Being extremely perceptive by nature, the Labrador is able to sense human moods almost

Tributes to the Breed

instantaneously. In black moments, when everything seems to be going wrong, he has a very amusing way of showing his affection that cannot help but bring a smile.

All Labrador fans should be especially proud of the way in which the breed has distinguished itself in extracurricular activities. In World War II the Labrador gained the reputation of being able to detect land mines in less time and with more intelligence than any other breed. They have performed so successfully as guide dogs for the blind that today they are among the three most preferred breeds.

Properly cared for and trained, your Labrador Retriever will be a most obedient and pleasant companion in the house and outdoors in all sorts of weather, and in or out of the water. His short, oily coat protects him from the cold and enables him to dry off quickly.

Feeding

Now let's talk about feeding your dog, a subject so simple that it's amazing there is so much nonsense and misunderstanding about it. Is it expensive to feed a dog? No, it is not! You can feed your dog economically and keep him in perfect shape the year round, or you can feed him expensively. He'll thrive either way, and let's see why this is true.

First of all, remember a dog is a dog. Dogs do not have a high degree of selectivity in their food, and unless you spoil them with great variety (and possibly turn them into poor, "picky" eaters) they will eat almost anything that they become accustomed to. Many dogs flatly refuse to eat nice, fresh beef. They pick around it and eat everything else. But meat—bah! Why? They aren't accustomed to it! They are hounds. They'd eat rabbit fast enough, but they refuse beef because they aren't used to it.

Variety Not Necessary

A good general rule of thumb is forget all about human preferences and don't give a thought to variety. Choose the right diet for your dog and feed it to him day after day, year after year, winter and summer. But what is the right diet?

Hundreds of thousands of dollars have been spent in canine nutrition research. The results are pretty conclusive, so you needn't go into a lot of experimenting with trials of this and that every other week. Research has proven just what your dog needs to eat and to keep healthy.

Dog Food

There are almost as many right diets as there are dog experts, but the basic diet most often recommended is one that consists of a dry food, either meal or kibble form. There are several of these of excellent quality, manufactured by reliable concerns, research tested, and nationally advertised. They are inexpensive, highly satisfactory, and easily available in stores everywhere in containers of five to fifty pounds. Larger amounts cost less per pound, usually.

Feeding

If you have a choice of brands, it is usually safer to choose the better-known one; but even so, carefully read the analysis on the package. Do not choose any food in which the protein level is less than 25 percent, and be sure that this protein comes from both animal *and* vegetable sources. The good dog foods have meat meal, fish meal, liver, and such, plus protein from alfalfa and soybeans, as well as some dried-milk product. Note the vitamin content carefully. See that they are all there in good proportions; and be especially certain that the food contains properly high levels of vitamins A and D, two of the most perishable and important ones. Note the B-complex level, but don't worry about carbohydrate and mineral levels. These substances are plentiful and cheap and not likely to be lacking in a good brand.

The advice given for how to choose a dry food also applies to moist or canned types of dog foods, if you decide to feed one of these.

Having chosen a really good food, feed it to your dog as the manufacturer directs. And once you've started, stick to it. Never change if you can possibly help it. A switch from one meal or kibble-type food can usually be made without too much upset; however, a change will almost invariably give you (and the dog) some trouble.

Fat Important; Meat Optional

While the better dog foods are complete in themselves in every respect, there is one item to add to the food, and that is *fat*—any kind of melted animal fat. It can be lard, bacon, or ham fat or from beef, lamb, pork, or poultry. A grown dog should have at least a tablespoon or two of melted fat added to one feeding a day. If you feed your dog morning and night, give him half of the fat in each feeding.

The addition of meat to this basic ration is optional. There is a sufficient amount of everything your dog needs already in the food, but you may add any meat you wish, say, a half to a quarter of a pound. In adding meat, the glandular meats are best, such as kidneys, pork liver, and veal or beef heart. They are all cheap to buy and are far higher sources of protein than the usual muscle meat humans insist on. Cook these meats slightly or feed them raw. Liver and kidney should be cooked a little and fed sparingly since they are laxative to some dogs. Heart is ideal, raw or cooked. Or you can feed beef, lamb, ocean fish well cooked, and pork.

Feeding

When Supplements Are Needed

Now what about supplements of various kinds, mineral and vitamin, or the various oils? They are all okay to add to your dog's food. However, if you are feeding your dog a correct diet, and this is easy to do, no supplements are necessary unless your dog has been improperly fed, has been sick, or is having puppies. Vitamins and minerals are naturally present in all foods; and to ensure against any loss through processing, they are added in concentrated form to the dog food you use. Except on the advice of your veterinarian, extra and added amounts of vitamins can prove harmful to your dog! The same risk goes with minerals.

Feeding Schedule

When and how much food to give your dog? As to when (except in the instance of puppies which will be taken up later), suit yourself. You may feed two meals per day or the same amount in one single feeding, either morning or night. As to how to prepare the food and how much to give, it is generally best to follow the directions on the food package. Your own dog may want a little more or a little less.

Fresh, cool water should always be available to your dog. This is important to good health throughout his lifetime.

All Dogs Need to Chew

Puppies and young dogs need something with resistance to chew on while their teeth and jaws are developing—for cutting the puppy teeth, to induce growth of the permanent teeth under the puppy teeth, to assist in getting rid of the puppy teeth at the proper time, to help the permanent teeth through the gums, to ensure normal jaw development, and to settle the permanent teeth solidly in the jaws.

The adult dog's desire to chew stems from the instinct for tooth cleaning, gum massage, and jaw exercise—plus the need for an outlet for periodic doggie tensions.

This is why dogs, especially puppies and young dogs, will often destroy property worth hundreds of dollars when their chewing instinct is not diverted from their owner's possessions. And this is why you should provide your dog with something to chew—something that

Feeding

has the necessary functional qualities, is desirable from the dog's viewpoint, and is safe for your dog.

It is very important that dogs not be permitted to chew on anything they can break or on any indigestible thing from which they can bite sizeable chunks. Sharp pieces, such as from a bone which can be broken by a dog, may pierce the intestinal wall and kill. Indigestible things which can be bitten off in chunks, such as from shoes or rubber or plastic toys, may cause an intestinal stoppage (if not regurgitated) and bring painful death, unless surgery is promptly performed.

Strong natural bones, such as 4- to 8-inch lengths of round shin bone from mature beef—either the kind you can get from a butcher or one of the variety available commercially in pet stores—may serve your dog's teething needs if his mouth is large enough to handle them effectively. You may be tempted to give your puppy a smaller bone and he may not be able to break it when you do, but puppies grow rapidly and the power of their jaws constantly increases until maturity. This means that a growing dog may break one of the smaller bones at any time, swallow the pieces, and die painfully before you realize what is wrong.

All hard natural bones are highly abrasive. If your dog is an avid chewer, natural bones may wear away his teeth prematurely; hence, they then should be taken away from your dog when the teething purposes have been served. The badly worn, and usually painful, teeth of many mature dogs can be traced to excessive chewing on natural bones.

Contrary to popular belief, knuckle bones which can be chewed up and swallowed by the dog provide little, if any, useable calcium or other nutriment. They do, however, disturb the digestion of most dogs and cause them to vomit the nourishing food they need.

Dried rawhide products of various types, shapes, sizes, and prices are available on the market and have become quite popular. However, they don't serve the primary chewing functions very well; they are a bit messy when wet from mouthing, and most dogs chew them up rather rapidly—but they have been considered safe for dogs until recently. Now, more and more incidents of death, and near death, by strangulation have been reported to be the result of partially swallowed chunks of rawhide swelling in the throat. More

Feeding

recently, some veterinarians have been attributing cases of acute constipation to large pieces of incompletely digested rawhide in the intestine.

The nylon bones, especially those with natural meat and bone fractions added, are probably the most complete, safe, and economical answer to the chewing need. Dogs cannot break them or bite off sizeable chunks; hence, they are

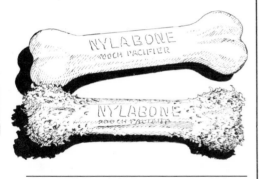

The upper Nylabone has not yet been chewed; the lower Nylabone shows normal signs of wear.

completely safe—and being longer lasting than other things offered for the purpose, they are economical.

Hard chewing raises little bristle-like projections on the surface of the nylon bones—to provide effective interim tooth cleaning and vigorous gum massage, much in the same way your toothbrush does it for you. The little projections are raked off and swallowed in the form of thin shavings, but the chemistry of the nylon is such that they break down in the stomach fluids and pass through without effect.

The toughness of the nylon provides the strong chewing resistance needed for important jaw exercise and effectively aids teething functions, but there is no tooth wear because nylon is non-abrasive. Being inert, nylon does not support the growth of microorganisms; and it can be washed in soap and water or it can be sterilized by boiling or in an autoclave.

Nylabone® is highly recommended by veterinarians as a safe, healthy nylon bone that can't splinter or chip. Nylabone® is frizzled by the dog's chewing action, creating a toothbrush-like surface that cleanses the teeth and massages the gums. Nylabone® and Nylaball,® the only chew products made of flavor-impregnated solid nylon, are available in your local pet shop.

Nothing, however, substitutes for periodic professional attention to your dog's teeth and gums, not any more than your toothbrush can do that for you. Have your dog's teeth cleaned by your veterinarian at least once a year (twice a year is better) and he will be healthier, happier, and far more pleasant to live with.

Training

You owe proper training to your dog. The right and privilege of being trained is his birthright; and whether your dog is going to be a handsome, well-mannered housedog and companion, a show dog, or whatever possible use he may be put to, the basic training is always the same—all must start with basic obedience, or what might be called "manners training."

Your dog must come instantly when called and obey the "Sit" or "Down" command just as fast; he must walk quietly at "Heel," whether on or off the lead. He must be mannerly and polite wherever he goes; he must be polite to strangers on the street and in stores. He must be orderly in the presence of other dogs. He must not bark at children on roller skates, motorcycles, or domestic animals. And he must be restrained from chasing cats. It is not a dog's inalienable right to chase cats, and he must be reprimanded for it.

Professional Training

How do you go about this training? Well, it's a very simple procedure, pretty well standardized by now. First, if you can afford the extra expense, you may send your dog to a professional trainer, where in 30 to 60 days he will learn how to be a "good dog." If you enlist the services of a good professional trainer, follow his advice about when to come to see the dog. No, he won't forget you, but too-frequent visits at the wrong time may slow down his training progress. And using a "pro" trainer means you will have to go for some training, too, after the trainer feels your dog is ready to go home. You will have to learn how your dog works, just what to expect of him and how to use what the dog has learned after he is home.

Obedience Training Class

Another way to train your dog (many experienced dog people think this is the best) is to join an obedience-training class right in your own community. There is such a group in nearly every community nowadays. Here you will be working with a group of people who are also just starting out. You will actually be training your own dog, since all work is done under the direction of a head trainer who will make suggestions to you and also tell you when and how to correct your dog's errors. Then, too, working with such a group, your dog will learn to get along with other dogs. And, what is more important, he will learn to do exactly what he is told to do, no matter how much confusion there is around him or how great the temptation to go his own way.

Write to your national kennel club for the location of a training club or class in your locality. Sign up. Go to it regularly—every session! Go early and leave late! Both you and your dog will benefit tremendously.

Train Him By The Book

The third way of training your dog is by the book. Yes, you can do it this way and do a good job of it too. If you can read and if you're smarter than the dog, you'll do a good job. But in using the book method, select a book, buy it, study it carefully; then study it some more, until the procedures are almost second nature to you. *Then* start your training. But stay with the book and its advice and exercises. Don't start in and then make up a few rules of your own. If you don't follow the book, you'll get into jams you can't get out of by yourself. If after a few hours of short training sessions your dog is

still not working as he should, get back to the book for a study session, because it's *your* fault, not the dog's! The procedures of dog training have been so well systematized that it must be your fault, since literally thousands of fine dogs have been trained by the book.

After your dog is "letter perfect" under all conditions, then, if you wish, go on to advanced training and trick work.

Your dog will love his obedience training, and you'll burst with pride at the finished product! Your dog will enjoy life even more, and you'll enjoy your dog more. And remember—you *owe* good training to your dog!

There are a number of good books that give detailed training information.

Showing

A show dog is a comparatively rare thing. He is one out of several litters of puppies. He happens to be born with a degree of physical perfection that closely approximates the standard by which the breed is judged in the show ring. Such a dog should, at maturity, be able to win or approach his championship in good, fast company at the larger shows. Upon finishing his championship, he is apt to be highly desirable as a breeding animal. As a proven stud, he will automatically command a high price for service.

Showing dogs is a lot of fun—yes, but it is a highly competitive sport. Though all the experts were once beginners, the odds are against a novice. You will be showing against experienced handlers, both pro and amateur, people who have devoted a lifetime to breeding, picking the right ones, and then showing those dogs through to their championships. Moreover, the most perfect dog ever born has faults, and in your hands the faults will be far more evident than with the experienced handler who knows how to minimize his dog's faults. There are but a few points on the sad side of the picture.

The experienced handler, however, was not born knowing the ropes. He learned—*and so can you!* You can if you will put in the same time, study, and keen observation that he did. But it will take time!

Key to Success

First, search for a truly fine show-prospect puppy. Take the puppy home, raise him by the book, and, as carefully as you know how, give him every chance to mature into the dog hoped for. Some dog experts recommend keeping a show-prospect puppy out of big shows, even Puppy Classes, until he is mature. When he is approaching maturity, break him in at match shows (more on these later); after this experience for the dog and you, then go gunning for the big wins at the big shows.

Showing

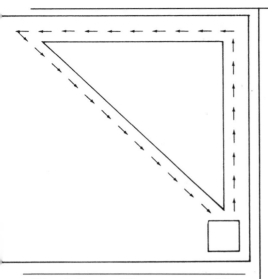

Although there are different patterns to follow when gaiting your dog, this is the one most frequently used.

Next step: read the standard by which the breed is judged. Study it until you know it by heart. Having done this—and while your puppy is at home (where he should be) growing into a fine normal, healthy dog—go to every dog show you can possibly reach. Sit at the ringside and watch the judging. Keep your ears and eyes open. Do your own judging, holding each of those dogs against the standard, which you now know by heart.

In your evaluations, don't start off looking for faults. Look for the virtues—the best qualities. How does a given dog shape up against the standard? Having looked for and noted the virtues, then note the faults and see what prevents a given dog from standing correctly or moving well. Weigh these faults against the virtues, since, ideally, every feature of the dog should contribute to the harmonious whole.

"Ringside Judging"

It's a good practice to make notes on each dog, always holding the dog against the standard. In "ringside judging," forget your personal preference for this or that feature. What does the standard say about it? Watch carefully as the judge places the dogs in a given class. It is difficult from the ringside always to see why number one was placed over the second dog. Try to follow the judge's reasoning. Later try to talk with the judge after he is finished (not every judge will have the time or inclination for this). Ask him questions as to why he placed certain dogs and not others. Listen while the judge explains his placings.

When you're not at the ringside, talk with the fanciers and breeders. Don't be afraid to ask opinions or say that you don't know. You have a lot of listening to do, and it will help you a great deal and speed up

Showing

your personal progress if you are a good listener.

Join the Clubs

You will find it worthwhile to join the national kennel club, which is the governing body for all purebred dogs in a particular country, and to subscribe to its magazine, if one is published. From this national kennel club, you can learn the location of the national breed club (known as the "parent club" for that breed), which you also should join. Being a member of these clubs will afford you the opportunity to get to know other people who share your interests and concerns, to learn more about your breed, and to find out when and where match shows and point shows will be held.

For information regarding sanctioned shows in most English-speaking areas, write to one of the kennel clubs listed below:

American Kennel Club
51 Madison Avenue
New York, NY 10010
USA

Australian Kennel Club
Royal Show Grounds
Ascot Vale, Victoria
Australia

British Kennel Club
1 Clarges Street
London 41Y 8AB
England

Canadian Kennel Club
2150 Bloor Street West
Toronto, Ontario M6S 4V7
Canada

Irish Kennel Club
23 Earlsfort Terrace
Dublin 2
Ireland

Prepare for the Show

The first thing you must do to prepare for a show is to find out the dates and rules of the show you intend to attend. Write to the national kennel club and get a copy of their show dates and rules (and rules for obedience competition or field trials or whatever type of competition you are interested in).

You also must teach your dog and yourself some basics of dog showing. You must learn to "stack" your dog, and your dog must learn to stay in this show stance whenever required to do so. Your dog must learn to accept being examined by a stranger (in other words, the judge at the show). You will have to learn how to gait your dog, and your dog

Showing

must learn how to move properly at your side.

Enter Match Shows

Match shows differ from regular shows only in that no championship points are given. These shows are especially designed to launch young dogs (and young handlers) on a show career.

With the ring deportment you have watched at big shows firmly in mind and practice, enter your dog in as many match shows as you can. When in the ring, you have two jobs. One is to see to it that your dog is always being seen to best advantage. The other job is to keep your eye on the judge to see what he may want you to do next. Watch only the judge and your dog. Be quick and be alert; do exactly as the judge directs. Don't speak to him except to answer his questions. If he does something you don't like, don't say so. And don't irritate the judge (and everybody else) by constantly talking and fussing with your dog.

In moving about the ring, remember to keep clear of dogs beside you or in front of you. Many dog fanciers feel that you should *not* show your dog in a regular point show until he is at least close to maturity and after both you and he have had time to perfect ring manners and poise in the match shows.

Point Shows

Point shows are for purebred dogs registered with the club that is sanctioning the show. Each dog is entered in the show class which is appropriate for his age, sex, and previous show record. The show classes usually include Puppy, Novice, Bred-by-Exhibitor, American-bred, and Open; and there may also be a Veterans Class and Brace and Team Classes, among others.

There also may be a Junior Showmanship Class, a competition for youngsters. Young people between the ages of 10 and 16, inclusively, compete to see who best handles their dog, rather than to see which dog is best, as is done in the other classes.

For a complete discussion of show dogs, dog shows, and showing a dog, read *Successful Dog Show Exhibiting* by Anna Katherine Nicholas (T.F.H. Publications, Inc.).

Breeding

So you have a female dog and you want to breed her for a litter of puppies. Wonderful idea—very simple—lots of fun—make a lot of money. Well, it *is* a wonderful idea, but stop right there. It's not very simple—and you won't make a lot of money. Having a litter of puppies to bring up is

The external skeletal parts of a dog: 1. Cranium. 2. Cervical vertebra. 3. Thoracic vertebra. 4. Rib. 5. Lumber vertebra. 6. Ilium. 7. Femur. 8. Fibula. 9. Tibia. 10. Tarsus. 11. Metatarsus. 12. Phalanges. 13. Phalanges. 14. Ulna. 15. Radius. 16. Humerus. 17. Scapula.

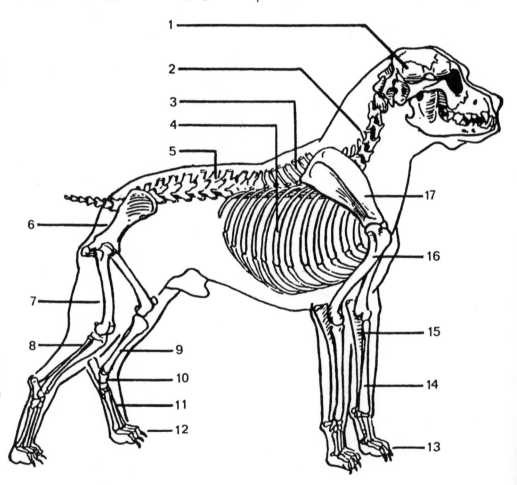

Breeding

hard, painstaking, thoughtful work; and only a few people regard such work as fun.

Breed Better Dogs

Bear in mind this very important point: Being a dog breeder is not just breeding dear Tillie to that darned good-looking male down the street. Would that it were that simple! Such a breeding will undoubtedly produce puppies. But that is not all you want. When you breed your female, it is only after the most careful planning—with every effort being made to be sure that the resulting puppies will be even better than the parent dogs (that they will come even closer to the standard than the parent animals) and that all the puppies will have good homes. Any fool can breed a litter of puppies; but only a careful, thoughtful, intelligent person can breed a litter of better puppies of your breed of dog. That must be your goal in breeding!

You can become a good novice breeder if you truly love the breed and are seriously concerned with the past, present, and future of the breed. You will breed your female only according to established scientific principles. Your personal sentiments have no place in the careful planning that goes on before you actually breed your female. The science of mammalian genetics is not a precise science like, say, mathematics. And the extensive reading you will do on the science (or art) of breeding dogs before you start to choose a stud will give you some idea of the variable factors you will be dealing with. It is a vast subject; but with the few brief pointers given here and additional reading and study, you can at least start on the right track.

Plan It on Paper

The principles of animal breeding are the same, whether the subjects be beef cattle, poultry, or dogs. To quote a cattle breeder, every breeding is first made "on paper" and later in the barnyard. In other words, first the blood strains of the animals are considered as to what goes well with what, so far as recorded ancestry is concerned. Having worked this out, the two animals to be mated must be studied and compared. If one does not excel where the other is lacking, at least in most points, then the paper planning must start over again and different animals be considered.

Breeding

With your own dog, there are several "musts" that are really axioms. First, breed only the best to the best. Two inferior animals will produce nothing but inferior animals, as surely as night follows day. To breed an inferior dog to another inferior one is a crime against the breed. So start by breeding the best to the best. And here again, an accurate knowledge of the standard is essential to know just what is best.

"Compensation" Breeding

No perfect dog has yet been whelped. Your female may be a winning show dog. She may be a champion. But she does have faults. In breeding her to a fine male, you must consider "compensation" breeding. She must compensate for his shortcomings and he for hers. For example, your female may be ideal in most respects but have faulty feet. So the male you choose, however ideal in other respects, *must* have ideal feet, as had his sire and dam too. In this way you may overcome the foot faults in your female's puppies.

This same principle applies to the correction of faults in any section of either male or female. But, you say, my dog has a pedigree as long as your arm. Must be good! Sad but true, a pedigree will not necessarily produce good puppies. A pedigree is no more—and no less—than your dog's recorded ancestry. Yes, you must know what dogs are in your dog's pedigree, but the most important point is, Were they good dogs? What were their faults and virtues? And to what degree did these dogs transmit these faults and virtues?

Breeding Methods

Now you may have heard that "like begets like." This is true and it is also false! Likes can beget likes only when both parent animals have the same likeness through generations of both family lines. The only way known to "fix" virtues and to eliminate faults is to mate two dogs of fairly close relationship bloodwise, two dogs which come from generations of likes and are family-related in their likeness. In this way you may ensure a higher and regular percentage of puppies which can be expected to mature into adults free at least from major faults under the standard. The likes must have the same genetic inheritance.

Through this "family" breeding, or line-breeding, correct type is set

Care of Mother and Family

and maintained. If both family lines are sound to begin with, family breeding and even close inbreeding (mating closely related dogs such as father and daughter) will merely improve the strain—but only in skilled hands. "Outcrossing" is mating dogs of completely different bloodlines with no, or only a few, common ancestors; it is used when undesirable traits begin to haunt closer breeding or when the breeder wants to bring in a specific trait or feature. The finest dogs today are the result of just such breeding methods. Study, expert advice, and experience will enable you, a novice, to follow these principles. So in your planning, forget the old nonsense about idiots and two-headed monsters coming from closely related parents.

Then, too, in your planning and reading, remember that intangible virtues, as well as physical ones, are without doubt inherited, as are faults in those intangibles. For example, in breeding bird dogs, where "nose sense" is of greatest importance, this factor can to a degree be fixed for future generations of puppies when the ancestors on both sides have the virtue of "nose sense." Just so, other characteristics of disposition or temperament can be fixed.

Let us assume that you have selected the right stud dog for your female and that she has been bred. In some 58 to 63 days, you will be presented with a nice litter of puppies. But there are a number of things to be gone over and prepared for in advance of the whelping date.

Before your female was bred, she was, of course, checked by your veterinarian and found to be in good condition and free from worms of any sort. She was in good weight but not fat. Once your female has been bred, you should keep your veterinarian informed of your female's progress; and when the whelping is imminent, your vet should be informed so that he can be on call in case any problems arise.

There's an old saying, "A litter should be fed from the day the bitch is bred," and there is a world of truth in it. So from the day your female is bred right up to the time the puppies are fully weaned, the mother's food is of the greatest importance. Puppies develop very rapidly in their 58 to 63 days of gestation, and their demands on the mother's system for nourishment are great. In effect, you are feeding your female and one to six or more other dogs, all at the same time.

Care of Mother and Family

The color captions for pages 57-64 can be found on page 16.

Additions to Regular Diet

For the first 21 days, your female will need but few additions to her regular diet. Feed her as usual, except for the addition of a small amount of "pot " or cottage cheese. This cheese, made from sour milk, is an ideal, natural source of added protein, calcium, and phosphorus—all essential to the proper growth of the unborn litter. Commercial vitamin-mineral supplements are unnecessary if the mother is fed the proper selection of natural foods.

Most commercial supplements are absolutely loaded with mineral calcium. You will usually find that the bulk of the contents is just plain calcium, a cheap and plentiful substance. Some dog experts believe, however, that calcium from an animal source like cheese is far more readily assimilated, and it is much cheaper besides. At any rate, do not use a commercial supplement without consulting your veterinarian and telling him the diet your dog is already getting.

Increase Food Intake

Along about the fifth week, the litter will begin to show a little, and now is the time to start an increase in food intake, not so much in bulk as in nutritive value. The protein content of your female's regular diet should be increased by the addition of milk products (cottage cheese, for example) meat (cooked pork liver, raw beef or veal heart, or some other meat high in protein), and eggs (either the raw yolk alone or, if the white is used, the egg should be cooked). Meanwhile, high-calorie foods should be decreased. The meat, cut into small pieces or ground, can be added to the basic ration. Mineral and vitamin supplements and cod-liver oil or additional fat also can be given to the female at this point, if your veterinarian so recommends.

Feed Several Times A Day

By now, your female is but a few weeks away from her whelping date, and the growing puppies are compressing her internal organs to an uncomfortable degree. She will have to relieve herself with greater frequency now. The stomach, too, is being compressed, so try reducing

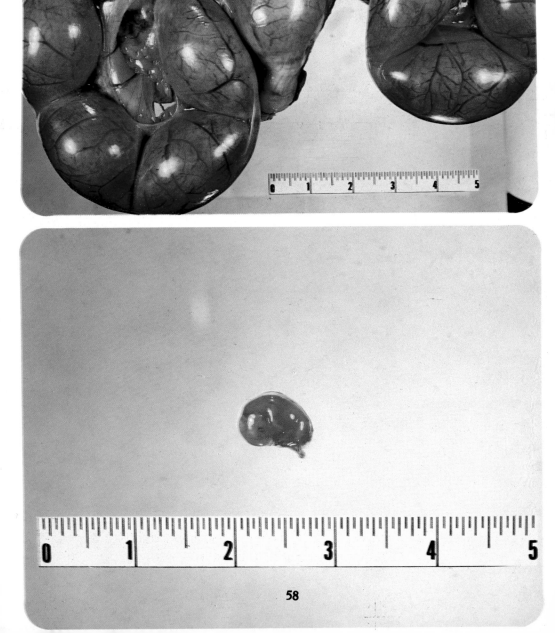

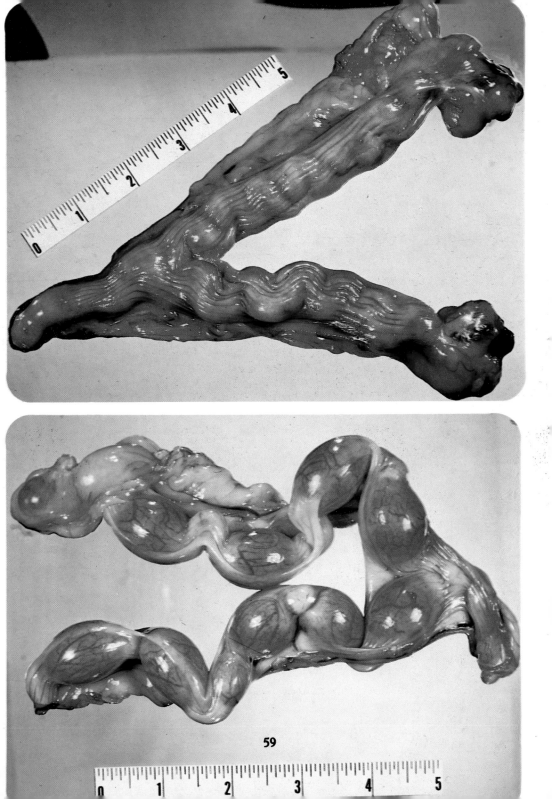

59

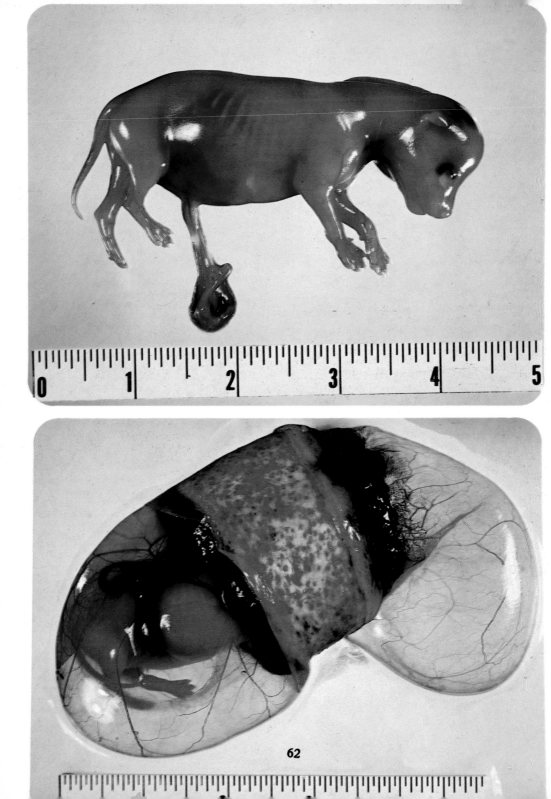

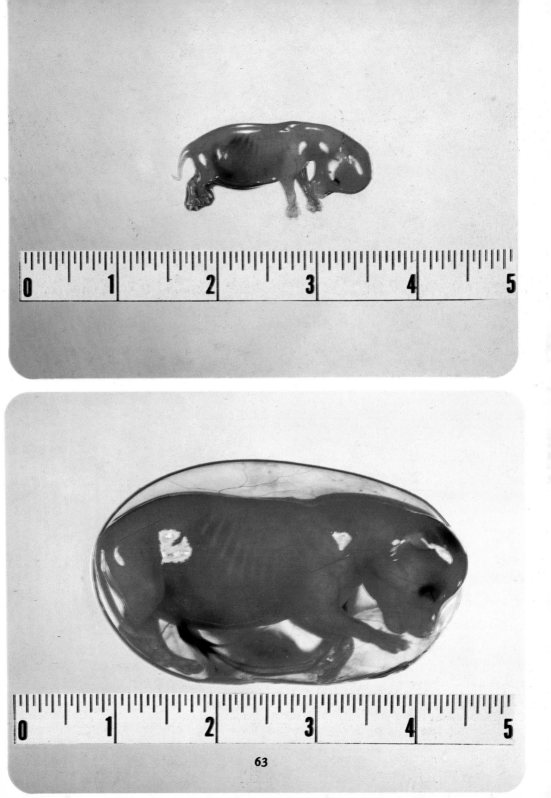

Care of Mother and Family

the basic ration slightly and at the same time increasing the meats, eggs, and milk products. Feed several small meals per day in order to get in the proper, stepped-up quantity of food without causing the increased pressure of a single large meal. The bitch should be fed generously, but she should not be allowed to become overweight.

Regular Exercise Important

A great deal of advice has been given by experts on keeping the female quiet from the day she is bred all through the pregnancy. Such quiet, however, is not natural and it cannot be enforced. Naturally, the female should not be permitted to go in for fence jumping; but she will be as active as ever during the first few weeks and gradually she will, of her own accord, slow down appropriately, since no one knows quite as much about having puppies as the dog herself—up to a point. But see to it that your female has plenty of gentle exercise all along. She'll let you know when she wants to slow down.

The color captions for pages 57-64 can be found on page 16.

Treat her normally, and don't let her be the victim of all the sentimentality that humans with impending families are heir to.

Whelping Imminent

About the morning of the 58th day or shortly thereafter, your female, who now looks like an outsize beer barrel, will suddenly refuse her food. She may drink water, however. If you have been observant as things progressed, your hand, if not your eye, will tell you that the litter has dropped. The female now has a saggy abdomen, and this is the tip-off that whelping will occur soon, usually well within the next 24 hours. As the actual whelping hour approaches, the mother will become increasingly restless. She will seek out dark places like closets. She will scratch at the floor and wad up rugs as if making a bed. She is pretty miserable right now, so be gently sympathetic with her but *not maudlin!*

Get her to stay in the whelping box you have had prepared for several days. The floor of the box should be covered with an old blanket or towel so that she will feel comfortable there. When the whelping starts, replace the bedding

Care of Mother and Family

with newspapers; these can be replaced as they get scratched up or soiled.

The whelping box should be located in a warm, not hot, place free from drafts. The area should also be fairly quiet. You may, if you wish, confine her to the box by hitching her there with a leash to a hook three or four feet off the floor so she won't get twisted up in it. But when actual whelping starts, take off both leash and collar. Then, get yourself a chair and prepare for an all-night vigil. Somehow puppies always seem to be born at night, and the process is good for 12 to 14 hours usually.

Labor Begins

Stay with her when she starts to whelp, you and one other person she knows well and who is an experienced breeder. No audience, please! A supply of warm water, old turkish towels, and plenty of wiping rags are in order at this point.

When labor commences, the female usually assumes a squatting position, although some prefer to lie down. The first puppy won't look much like a puppy to you when it is fully expelled from the female. It will be wrapped in a dark, membranous sac, which the mother will tear open with her teeth, exposing one small, noisy pup—very wet. Let the mother lick the puppy off and help to dry it. She will also bite off the navel cord. This may make the puppy squeal, but don't worry, mama is not trying to eat her pup. The mother may eat a few of the sacs; this is normal. When she is through cleaning the puppy off, pick up the puppy and gently but firmly give it a good rubbing with a turkish towel. Do this in full sight of the mother and close enough so that she will not leave her whelping box.

When the puppy is good and dry and "squawking" a bit, place it near the mother or in a shallow paper box close to the mother so she can see it but will not step on it when she becomes restless with labor for the second puppy. If the room temperature is lower than 70 degrees, place a hot-water bottle wrapped in a towel near the puppies. Be sure to keep the water changed and warm so the puppies aren't lying on a cold water bottle. Constant warmth is essential.

Most dogs are easy whelpers, so you need not anticipate any trouble. Just stay with the mother, more as an observer than anything else. The experienced breeder who is keeping you company, or your vet, should handle any problems that arise.

66

Care of Mother and Family

Post-natal Care

When you are reasonably certain that the mother has finished whelping, have your veterinarian administer the proper amount of obstetrical pituitrin. This drug will induce labor again, thus helping to expel any retained afterbirth or dead puppy.

Inspect your puppies carefully. Rarely will any deformities be found; but if there should be any, make a firm decision to have your veterinarian destroy the puppy or puppies showing deformities.

During and after whelping, the female is very much dehydrated, so at frequent intervals she should be offered lukewarm milk or meat soup, slightly thickened with well-soaked regular ration. She will relish liquids and soft foods for about 24 hours, after which she will go back to her regular diet. But be sure she has a constant supply of fresh water available. Feed her and keep her water container outside the whelping box.

After all of the puppies have been born, the mother might like to go outside for a walk. Allow her this exercise. She probably won't want to be away from her puppies more than a minute or two.

The puppies will be blind for about two weeks, with the eyes gradually opening up at that time. The little pups will be quite active and crawl about over a large area. Be sure that all of the puppies are getting enough to eat. If the mother sits or stands, instead of lying still to nurse, the probable cause is scratching from the puppies nails. You can remedy this by clipping them, as you do hers.

Weaning Time

Puppies can usually be completely weaned at six weeks of age, although you can start to feed them at three weeks. They will find it easier to lap semi-solid food. At four weeks they should be given four meals a day, and soon they will do without their mother entirely. Start them on mixed dog food, or leave it with them in a dish for self-feeding. Don't leave water with them all the time; at this age everything is to play with and they will use it as a wading pool. They can drink all they need if it is offered several times a day, after meals.

As the puppies grow up, the mother will go into the box only to nurse them, first sitting up and then standing. The periods of time between the mother's visits to the box will gradually lengthen, until it is no longer necessary for her to nurse the pups.

Health and Disease

First, don't be frightened by the number of health problems that a dog might have over the course of his life-time. The majority of dogs never have any of them. Don't become a dog-hypochondriac. All dogs have days when they feel lazy and want to lie around doing nothing. For the few problems that you might be concerned about, remember that your veterinarian is your dog's best friend. When you first get your puppy, select a veterinarian whom you have faith in. He will get to know your dog and will be glad to have you consult him for advice. A dog needs little medical care, but that little is essential to his good health and well-being. He needs a proper diet given at regular hours; clean, roomy housing; daily exercise; companionship and love; frequent grooming; and regular check-ups by your veterinarian.

Using a Thermometer and Giving Medicines

Almost every serious ailment shows itself by an increase in the dog's body temperature. If your dog acts lifeless, looks dull-eyed, and gives the impression of illness,

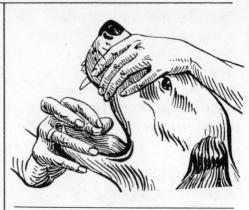

The proper way to give a pill or tablet.

check his temperature by using a rectal thermometer made of either plastic or glass. Hold the dog securely, insert the thermometer (which you have lubricated with petroleum jelly), and take a reading. The average normal temperature for your dog will be 101.5°F. Excitement may raise the temperature slightly; but any rise of

The proper way to give liquid medication.

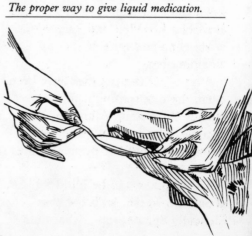

68

Health and Disease

more than a few points is cause for alarm, and your vet should be consulted.

Giving medicines to your dog is not really difficult. In order to administer a liquid medication, do not open the dog's mouth. Instead, form a pocket by pulling out the lower lip at the corner of the mouth; pour the medicine in with a spoon; hold the head only very slightly upward. (If the head is held too high, the medicine may enter the windpipe instead of the passage to the stomach, thus choking the dog.) With agitated animals, medicine can still be given by this method, even though the dog's mouth is held shut with a tape or a muzzle.

In order to administer a pill or tablet, raise your dog's head slightly and open his mouth. (Using one hand, grasp the cheeks of the dog, and then press inward. The pressure of the lips pushed against the teeth will keep the mouth open). With the other hand, place the pill or tablet far back on the middle of the tongue. Quickly remove your hand from the dog's cheeks; hold the dog's mouth closed (but not too tightly), and gently massage his throat. You can tell the medicine has been swallowed when the tip of the dog's tongue shows between his front teeth.

A Vaccination Schedule

Prevention is the key word for many dog diseases, and the best prevention is a series of vaccinations administered by your veterinarian. Such contagious diseases as distemper, hepatitis, parainfluenza, leptospirosis, rabies, and canine parvovirus can be virtually eliminated by strictly following a vaccination schedule.

Distemper is probably the most virulent of all dog diseases. Young dogs are most susceptible to it, although it may affect dogs of all ages. The dog will lose his appetite, seem depressed, feel chilled, and run a fever. Often he will have a watery discharge from his eyes and nose. Unless treated promptly, the disease goes into advanced stages with infections of the lungs, intestines, and nervous system; and dogs that recover may be left with some impairment such as paralysis, convulsions, a twitch, or some other defect, usually spastic in nature. The best protection against this is very early inoculation with a series of permanent shots and a booster shot each year thereafter.

Hepatitis is a viral disease spread by contact. The initial symptoms of drowsiness, vomiting, great thirst, loss of appetite, and a high temperature closely resemble those

Health and Disease

of distemper. These symptoms are often accompanied by swellings of the head, neck, and abdomen. The disease strikes quickly; death may occur in just a few hours. Protection is afforded by injection with a vaccine.

Parainfluenza is commonly called "kennel cough." Its main symptom is coughing; and since it is highly contagious, it can sweep through an entire kennel in just a short period of time. A vaccination is a dog's best protection against this respiratory disease.

Leptospirosis is caused by bacteria that live in stagnant or slow-moving water. It is carried by rats and mice, and infection is begun by the dog licking substances contaminated by the urine or feces of infected animals. The symptoms are diarrhea and a yellowish-brownish discoloration of the jaws, tongue, and teeth, caused by an inflammation of the kidneys. This disease can be cured if caught in time, but it is best to ward it off with a vaccine which your veterinarian can administer.

Rabies is an acute disease of the dog's central nervous system. It is spread by infectious saliva transmitted by the bite of an infected animal. Rabies is generally manifested in one or the other of two groups of symptoms, and the symptoms usually appear within five days. The first is "furious rabies," in which the dog exhibits changes in his personality. The dog becomes hypersensitive and runs at and bites everything in sight. Eventually, the animal's lower jaw becomes paralyzed and hangs down; he walks with a stagger and saliva drips from his mouth. The second syndrome is referred to as "dumb rabies" and is characterized by the dog's walking in a bearlike manner, head down. The lower jaw is paralyzed, and the dog is unable to bite. Outwardly, it may seem as though he has a bone caught in his throat.

Even if your pet should be bitten by a rabid dog or other animal, he probably can be saved if you get him to the veterinarian in time for a series of injections. However, after the symptoms have appeared, no cure is possible. Remember that an annual rabies inoculation is almost certain protection against rabies. If you suspect that your dog or some other animal has rabies, notify your local health department. A rabid animal is a danger to all who come near him.

Canine parvovirus is a highly contagious viral disease that attacks the intestinal tract, white blood cells, and less frequently the heart muscle. It is believed to spread through dog-to-dog contact (the

Health and Disease

specific source of infection being the fecal matter of infected dogs), but it can also be transmitted from place to place on the hair and feet of infected dogs and by contact with contaminated cages, shoes, and the like. It is particularly hard to overcome because it is capable of existing in the environment for many months under varying conditions, unless strong disinfectants are used.

The symptoms are vomiting, fever, diarrhea (often blood-streaked), depression, loss of appetite, and dehydration. Death may occur in only two days. Puppies are hardest hit, with the virus being fatal to 75 percent of the puppies that contact it. Older dogs fare better; the disease is fatal to only two to three percent of those afflicted.

The best preventive measure for parvovirus is vaccination administered by your veterinarian. Precautionary measures individual pet owners can take include disinfecting the kennel and other areas where the dog is housed. One part sodium hypochlorite solution (household bleach) to 30 parts of water will do the job efficiently. Keep the dog from coming into contact with the fecal matter of other dogs when walking or exercising your pet.

Internal Parasites

There are four common internal parasites that may infect your dog. These are roundworms, hookworms, whipworms, and tapeworms. The first three can be diagnosed by laboratory examination; the presence of tapeworms is determined by seeing segments in the stool or attached to the hair around the tail. Do not under any circumstances attempt to worm your dog without the advice of your veterinarian. After first determining what type of worm or worms are present, he will advise you of the best method of treatment.

A dog or puppy in good physical condition is less susceptible to worm infestation than a weak dog. Proper sanitation and a nutritious diet help in preventing worms. One of the best preventive measures is to always have clean, dry bedding for

Adult whipworms are between two and three inches long, and the body of each worm is no thicker than a heavy sewing needle.

Health and Disease

your dog. This will diminish the possibility of reinfection due to flea or tick bites.

Heartworm infestation in dogs is passed by mosquitoes and can be a life-threatening problem. Dogs with the disease tire easily, have difficulty breathing, cough, and may lose weight despite a hearty appetite. If caught in the early stages, the disease can be effectively treated; however, the administration of daily preventive medicine throughout the spring, summer, and fall months is strongly advised. Your veterinarian must first take a blood sample from your dog to test for the presence of the disease. If the dog is heartworm-free, pills or liquid medicine can be prescribed that will protect against any infestation.

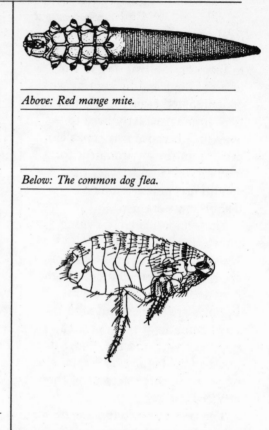

Above: Red mange mite.

Below: The common dog flea.

A female dog tick that is gorged with blood.

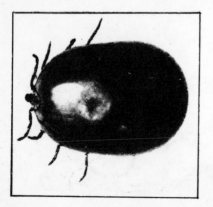

Below: The under side of a sarcoptic mange mite.

Health and Disease

External Parasites

Fleas and ticks are the two most common external parasites that can trouble a dog. Along with the general discomfort and irritation that they bring to a dog, these parasites can infest him with worms and disease. The flea is a carrier of tapeworm and may act as an intermediate host for heartworm. The tick can cause dermatitis and anemia, and it may also be a carrier of Rocky Mountain spotted fever and canine babesiasis, a blood infection. If your dog becomes infested with fleas, he should be treated with a medicated dip bath or some other medication recommended by your vet. Ticks should be removed with great care;

A sticktight flea.

you must be certain that the head of the tick is not left in the dog—this could be a source of infection.

Two types of mange, sarcoptic and follicular, are also caused by parasites. The former is by far the more common and results in an intense irritation, causing violent scratching. Close examination will reveal small red spots which become filled with pus. This is a highly

A female tick.

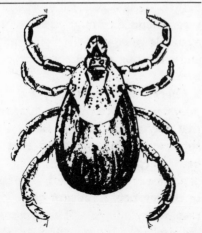

A male tick.

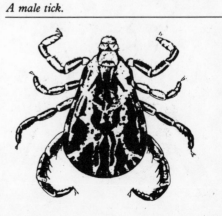

Health and Disease

contagious condition, and any dog showing signs of the disease should be isolated. Consult your veterinarian for the proper treatment procedures. Follicular mange is very much harder to cure; but fortunately, it is much rarer and less contagious. This disease will manifest itself as bare patches appearing in the skin, which becomes thickened and leathery. A complete cure from this condition is only rarely effected.

Other Health Problems

Hip dysplasia is an often crippling condition more prevalent in large

A dislocation of the upper leg bone. Dislocations should be immediately attended to by your vet.

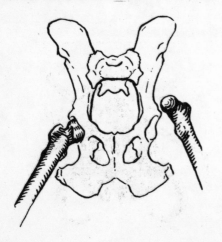

breeds than in small, but it has occurred in almost every breed. The cause is not known absolutely, though it is believed to be hereditary, and as yet there is no known cure. The condition exists in varying degrees of severity. In general, hip dysplasia can be described as a poor fit between the two bones of the hip joint and is caused by a malformation of one or the other. The condition causes stiffness in the hindlegs, considerable pain in the more severe cases, and difficulty of movement. It generally manifests itself in puppyhood and can be noticed by the time the young dog is two months old. If hip dysplasia is suspected, the dog should be x-rayed; and if afflicted, it should not be used for breeding. When the pain is severe and continual, euthanasia is occasionally recommended, though medication is available to control the pain and allow the dog to move with more ease.

Coughs, colds, bronchitis, and pneumonia are respiratory diseases that may affect the dog. Being subjected to cold or a draft after a bath, sleeping near an air conditioner or in the path of a fan, or resting near a radiator can cause respiratory ailments. The symptoms are similar to those in humans;

Health and Disease

however, the germs of these diseases are different and do not affect both dogs and humans, so they cannot be infected by each other. Treatment is much the same as for a child with the same type of illness. Keep the dog warm, quiet, and well fed. Your veterinarian has antibiotics and other remedies to help the dog recover.

Eczema is a disease that occurs most often in the summer months and affects the dog down the back, especially just above the root of the tail. It should not be confused with mange, as it is not caused by a parasite. One of the principle causes of eczema is improper nutrition, which makes the dog susceptible to disease. Hot, humid weather promotes the growth of bacteria, which can invade a susceptible dog and thereby cause skin irritation and lesions. It is imperative that the dog gets relief from the itching that is symptomatic of the disease, as self-mutilation by scratching will only help to spread the inflammation. Antibiotics may be necessary if a bacterial infection is, indeed, present.

Moist eczema, commonly referred to as "hot spots," is a rapidly appearing skin disease that produces a moist infection. Spots appear very suddenly and may spread rapidly in a few hours, infecting several parts of the body. These lesions are generally bacterially infected and are extremely itchy, which will cause the dog to scratch frantically and further damage the afflicted areas. Vomiting, fever, and an enlargement of the lymph nodes may occur. The infected areas must be clipped to the skin and thoroughly cleaned. Your veterinarian will prescribe an anti-inflammatory drug and antibiotics, as well as a soothing emollient to relieve itching.

The *eyes*, because of their sensitivity, are prone to injury and infection. Dogs that spend a great deal of time outdoors in heavily wooded areas may return from an exercise excursion with watery eyes, the result of brambles and high weeds scratching them. The eyes may also be irritated by dirt and other foreign matter. Should your dog's eyes appear red and watery, a mild solution can be mixed at home for a soothing washing. Your veterinarian will be able to tell you what percentage of boric acid, salt, or other medicinal compound to mix with water. You must monitor your dog's eyes after such a solution is administered; if the irritation persists, or if there is a significant discharge, immediate veterinary attention is warranted.

Your dog's *ears*, like his eyes, are extremely sensitive and can also be

Health and Disease

prone to infection, should wax and/or dirt be allowed to build up. Ear irritants may be present in the form of mites, soap or water, or foreign particles which the dog has come into contact with while romping through a wooded area. If your dog's ears are bothering him, you will know it—he will scratch his ears and shake his head, and the ears will have a foul-smelling dark secretion. This pasty secretion usually signals the onset of *otorrhea*, or ear canker, and at this stage proper veterinary care is essential if the dog's hearing is not to be permanently impaired. In the advanced stages of ear canker, tissue builds up within the ear, and the ear canal becomes blocked off, thus diminishing the hearing abilities of that ear. If this is to be prevented, you should wash your dog's ears, as they require it, with a very dilute solution of hydrogen peroxide and water, or an antibacterial ointment, as your vet suggests. In any case,

An ear mite.

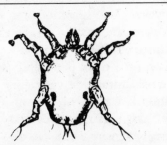

the ears, because of their delicacy, are to be washed gently, with a soft cloth or cotton.

Your pet's *teeth* can be maintained by his regular use of a chew product such as Nylabone® or Nylaball,® which serves to clean the teeth of tartar accumulation and to massage and stimulate the gums. Tartar accumulates on the teeth of dogs, particularly at the gum line, more rapidly than on the teeth of humans; and these accumulations, if not removed, bring irritation, infection and, ultimately, destruction of the teeth at the roots. With puppies, a chew product helps to relieve the discomfort of the teething stage and, of course, prevents the pup's chewing of your furniture and slippers! A periodic inspection of your dog's mouth will alert you to any problem he might have which would require a trip to the veterinarian's office. Any signs of tooth or gum sensitivity, redness, or swelling, signal the need for professional treatment.

A dog's *nails* should not be allowed to become overlong. If you live in a city and walk your dog regularly on pavement, chances are that his nails are kept trimmed from the "wear and tear" they receive from the sidewalks. However, if your dog gets all of his exercise in your yard, or if his nails simply

Health and Disease

grow rather quickly, it will occasionally be necessary for you to clip his nails. It is best for you to have your veterinarian show you the proper way to perform the nail clipping. Special care must always be taken to avoid cutting too far and reaching the "quick." If you cut into the quick of the nail, it will bleed, so it is easy to see why an expert must show you the proper procedure. A nail clipper designed especially for dogs can be purchased at any pet shop.

Emergency First Aid

If you fear that your dog has swallowed *poison*, immediately get him to the veterinarian's. Try to locate the source of poisoning; if he has swallowed, for example, a cleaning fluid kept in your house, check the bottle label to see if inducing the dog to vomit is necessary. Inducing the dog to vomit can be very harmful, depending upon the type of poison swallowed. Amateur diagnosis is very dangerous.

Accidents, unfortunately, do happen, so it is best to be prepared. If your dog gets hit by a car or has a bad fall, keep him absolutely quiet, move him as little as possible, and get veterinary treatment as soon

as possible. It is unwise to give any stimulants such as brandy or other alcoholic liquids when there is visible external hemorrhage or the possibility of internal hemorrhaging.

Minor cuts and wounds will be licked by your dog, but you should treat such injuries as you would your own. Wash out the dirt and apply an antiseptic.

Severe cuts and wounds should be bandaged as tightly as possible to stop the bleeding. A wad of cotton may serve as a pressure bandage, which will ordinarily stop the flow of blood. Gauze wrapped around the cotton will hold it in place. Usually applying such pressure to a wound will sufficiently stop the blood flow; however, for severe bleeding, such as when an artery is cut, a tourniquet may be necessary. Apply a tourniquet between the injury and the heart if the bleeding is severe. To tighten the tourniquet, push a pencil through the bandage and twist it. Take your dog to a veterinarian immediately, since a tourniquet should not be left in place any longer than fifteen minutes.

Minor burns or scalds can be treated by clipping hair away from the affected area and then applying a paste of bicarbonate of soda and water. Apply it thickly to the burned area and try to keep the dog

Care of the Oldster

from licking it off.

Serious burns require the immediate attention of your veterinarian, as shock quickly follows such a burn. The dog should be kept quiet, wrapped in a blanket; and if he still shows signs of being chilled, use a hot-water bottle. Clean the burn gently, removing any foreign matter such as bits of lint, hair, grass, or dirt; and apply cold compresses. Act as quickly as possible. Prevent exposure to air by covering with gauze, cotton, and a loose bandage. To prevent the dog from interfering with the dressing, muzzle him and have someone stay with him until veterinary treatment is at hand.

Stings from wasps and bees are a hazard for the many dogs that enjoy trying to catch these insects. A sting frequently follows a successful catch, and it often occurs inside the mouth, which can be very serious. The best remedy is to get him to a veterinarian as soon as possible, but there are some precautionary measures to follow in the meantime. If the dog has been lucky enough to be stung only on the outside of the face, try to extricate the stinger; then swab the point of entry with a solution of bicarbonate of soda. In the case of a wasp sting, use vinegar or some other acidic food.

Barring accident or disease, your dog is apt to enjoy a life of 12 to 14 years. However, beginning roughly with the eighth year, there will be a gradual slowing down. And with this there are many problems of maintaining reasonably good health and comfort for all concerned.

While there is little or nothing that can be done in the instance of failing sight and hearing, proper management of the dog can minimize these losses. Fairly close and carefully supervised confinement are necessary in both cases. A blind dog, otherwise perfectly healthy and happy, can continue to be happy if he is always on a leash outdoors and guided so that he does not bump into things. Indoors, he will do well enough on his own. Dogs that are sightless seem to move around the house by their own radar system. They learn where objects are located; but once they do learn the pattern, care must be taken not to leave a piece of furniture out of its usual place.

Deafness again requires considerable confinement, especially in regard to motor traffic and similar hazards; but deafness curtails the dog's activities much less than blindness. It is not necessary to send any dog to the Great Beyond

Care of the Oldster

because it is blind or deaf—if it is otherwise healthy and seems to enjoy life.

Teeth in the aging dog should be watched carefully, not only for the pain they may cause the dog but also because they may poison the system without any local infection or pain. So watch carefully, especially when an old dog is eating. Any departure from his usual manner should make the teeth suspect at once. Have your veterinarian check the teeth frequently.

His System Slows Down

As the dog ages and slows down in his physical activity, so his whole system slows down. With the change, physical functions are in some instances slowed and in others accelerated—in effect, at least.

For example, constipation may occur; and bowel movements may become difficult, infrequent, or even painful. Chronic constipation is a problem for your veterinarian to deal with; but unless it is chronic, it is easily dealt with by adding a little extra melted fat to the regular food. Do not increase roughage or administer physics unless so directed by your veterinarian. If the added

fat in the food doesn't seem to be the answer to occasional constipation, give your dog a half or a full teaspoon of mineral oil two or three times a week. Otherwise, call your veterinarian.

On either side of the rectal opening just below the base of the tail are located the two anal glands. Occasionally these glands do not function properly and may cause the dog great discomfort if not cleaned out. This is a job for your veterinarian, until after he has shown you how to do it.

Watch His Weight

In feeding the aging dog, try to keep his weight down. He may want just as much to eat as ever, but with

An easy way to weigh your dog is to hold the dog while you stand on a scale, and then subtract your weight from the total.

Care of the Oldster

decreased activity he will tend to put on weight. This weight will tend to slow down all other bodily functions and place an added strain on the heart. So feed the same diet as usual, but watch the weight.

Age, with its relaxing of the muscles, frequently makes an otherwise clean dog begin to misbehave in the house, particularly so far as urination is concerned. There is little that can be done about it, if your veterinarian finds there is no infection present, except to give your dog more frequent chances to urinate and move his bowels. It's just a little bit more work on your part to keep your old friend more comfortable and a "good" dog.

Let your dog exercise as much as he wants to without encouraging him in any violent play. If he is especially sluggish, take him for a walk on a leash in the early morning or late evening. Avoid exercise for him during the heat of the day. And in cold weather or rain, try a sweater on him when he goes out. It's not "sissy" to put a coat on an old dog. You and your veterinarian, working closely together, can give your dog added life and comfort. So consult your veterinarian often.

Occasionally in an old dog there is a problem of unpleasant smell, both bodily and orally. If this situation is acute, it is all but unbearable to have the dog around. But the situation can be corrected or at least alleviated with frequent and rather heavy dosing of chlorophyll. A good rubdown with one of the dry-shampoo products is also helpful.

When the End Comes

People who have dogs are sooner or later faced with the tragedy of losing them. It's tough business losing a dog, no matter how many you may have at one time. And one dog never takes the place of another—so don't expect it to. When you lose your dog, get another as quickly as you can. It does help a lot.

Keep your dog alive as long as he is happy and comfortable. Do everything you reasonably can to keep him that way. But when the sad time comes that he is sick, always uncomfortable, or in some pain, it is your obligation then to have him put away. It is a tough ordeal to go through, but you owe it to your old friend to allow him to go to sleep. And, literally, that's just what he does. Your veterinarian knows what to do. And your good old dog, without pain, fright, bad taste, or bad smells, will just drift to sleep.